Oynx
International Journal

Volume 2

Oynx

Copyright © 2016 by

All rights reserved. This book or any portion thereof may not be reproduced or used in any manner whatsoever without the express written permission of the publisher except for the use of brief quotations in a book review.

Cover design by Joe Geran

ISBN:
978-0-9966565-6-6 Jasmaya Productions and Publications 10000 E.Paseo San Ardo Tucson, Arizona, 85747

Contents

From the Editor.... 6
   Kambon Obayani-Editor 6

Zygote 8
   Lola Rainey 8

Single Fathers Raising Sons 9
   Schauntte Parker 9

And Swallow The Silence 10
   Lola Rainey 12

Parenting with a Purpose 13
   By Denise St Patrick-Bell, PhD 13

It is Expected of Parents 18
   King E Carter 18

Smalltalk with My Six Year-Old Daughter 35
   David Marquard 35

Post-Partum Black & Blue 36
   Lola Rainey 36

Illustration by Joe Geran: Spirits of the Wind 37

mariachi plaza adjacent 38
   Gloria Enedina Alvarez 39

HEARTS OF SAPPHIRE 40
   by Emory Holmes II 40

Checkers 49
   by Mark Thomson 49

The Passersby 51
   by Erica K. B. 51

A Sensorial Mecca 72
   by Mark Thomson 72

What I was supposed to be writing 74
   Maat em Maakheru Amen 74

Illustration by Joe Geran: Guardians of the Sea 75

Only Love	76
King E. Carter	76
Beauty is Not Monolithic	77
King Carter	77
The SS Pacifica	78
Cecilia Manguerra Brainard	78
Our Failure to Say Farewell	85
David Marquard	85
Pillow Talk	86
Lola Rainey	86
Pornosophy (rev.)	87
Martin Perlich	89
Illustration by Joe Geran: Willie Tucker	90
The Museum Visit These Many Years Later	91
Susan Booker Morris	91
[This is my first poem	92
since the snow began to fall]	92
Phillip B Middleton	92
Swamp Woman	93
Lola Rainey	94
Yesterday's News (Live)	95
Phillip B. Middleton	96
The Snapshot	97
by Pam Ward	97
The Death of the Truth About Death	109
Martin Perlich	110
Yeast	111
Kimberly Evans	113
I am clay	114
Azam Obidov	114
Perhaps, for Bulabeck Deng, a Dreamsong	115

- Phillip B Middleton 121
- God is sleeping 122
  - Azam Obidov 122
- Cartography in California 123
  - David Maruyama 133
- THE SERPENT IN THE BARN RAFTERS 134
  - George Edward Buggs 135
- THADDEUS GOTDOE pt2 136
- A tale of a vampire 136
  - John Dickson 151
- Illustration by Joe Geran: Brother Deacon Man 152
- DOO WOP DAZE DANCE 153
  - George Edward Buggs 154
- Upright Bass 155
  - Susan Booker Morris 155
- The Vampires Do the Ring Shout 156
- Down By the River 156
  - ////By Peter J. Harris////Copyright 2016 156
- Author Bios 182

From the Editor....

The second edition of Onyx International is Dedicated to Mel Taylor, author of the Mittman, and other unpublished novels (Sonny Boy's Last Dance, Pason' Blanc, This Secret), who transitioned in 2007, and with whom I spent countless hours reading works in progress to each other over the phone, sharing doing time tales, listening to music, discussing clothes, hustler's habits, writing, authors, and the "b", we called aging. He insisted on the sparsity of language, and knew that characters unseen, and not visualized, could never come alive on the page. I still grieve for him and miss his insights and sharing...Mel personified the saying "WHEN A WRITER DIES, A LIBRARY IS BURNED"...and many are burning...

The work, and the writers in this edition, are very much alive and their work is live embers smoldering in the word's fireplace, fragrant with seasoned metaphors and delicious insights..Sit with these wordsmiths at their table of tales, and partake in the poems and prose they've prepared for consumption.

Kambon Obayani-Editor

Zygote

The battle to survive. Starts in the womb.
The twinkling that is the beginning of something
splinters. Silken threads, sticky fine float across
the waters. Seeking squiggly egg bits. Bundled into sacs.
Look, see. A glycerin cradle. No sugar. Babe inside.
Why did you leave—sister?
Mama's hips were wide. Plenty room for two.
Did memories of muffled screams, ferment in the blood
a deading spell. To undo you?

Maybe. There was room for only one. Me.
Did I slay you—sister?
Exercise a queenly. Prerogative to purge. The tender self.
Or obliterate your sun. On the blunt edge of glacier will.
The mystery of your leaving. Is not without clues.
You disappeared into me. The way river cuts through rock. Bit by bit.
Not erasure. Garden alchemy. Orphan seeds sprouting. Unexpectedly.

Your hair, skin, teeth. Bud in my ovaries. Lungs, legs, arms inside my bones.
One day. You will emerge. Fully formed. I will depart. Retire to Mexico.
Change my name. Open a shop. Sell milagros to tourists.

Lola Rainey

Single Fathers Raising Sons

A single father never gets the respect that he is deserved. In my opinion a single father raising his son is a super hero that is invisible to the world. Of course most people can easily say "He just doing what he is supposed to do". Being on the outside looking in, that is a easy thing to say. You are not living in my skin. The sacrifices that a single father makes cannot be measured on the Richter scale. Before we go any further into being single and raising sons, let me give you a little background on my life before.

I can just imagine how many of you judgmental females and males will have to say about my life style as a Pimp. I lived on the top of the world like a superstar for years. Having it my way, and wanting for nothing. This journey started at the age of 19, and lasted for 30years. I raised my first son while I was in the life. He is now a teacher of Special Ed third grade students. His mother started using crack cocaine when he was three. Her addiction lasted until he was a senior in high school. All the important years of his life, I had to become mom, and dad. I have no regrets because I did what was necessary to make him become a better man than me. For that I thank God for the man that he became.

Judge all that you want, my life style had nothing to do with me being a single father doing what I had to do to make sure that my Son became the man that society wants, and needs.

I attribute my son's growth, the kind of man that he became, and his success in life, to one of the most precious treasure's that God has ever given all of us, LOVE that I gave him daily.

As a child growing up, I had two other brothers. Of course our parents loved us, but to take either of us in their arms and say "I love you", never took place. I raised my first son with hugging him every morning, after school, and before he went to bed. You would be surprised at how much a hug, and a I love you means to a child. Whether you realize it or not raising a man child on your own, love is essential in making him feel secure. I will tell you something very important. Once a man child reaches the age of twelve, if you don't continue to show him love, he will find it somewhere else. Gang bangers seek out man child. The love that is not given at home, will be given by them, so beware.

Single fathers raising sons must provide structure, love, strength, and a strong influence. These three keys of raising a man child will bring your son to respect you, and other adults that they come in contact with. Respect is so important especially from the age of twelve to eighteen. When Man Childs go into being teens, and after eighteen when they blossom into manhood. My grandparents used to call these years "The years are when boys are smelling themselves, and think that they know everything" I know that women will disagree with this statement but oh well. You can raise a man child but when he becomes a certain age he needs some type of, male figure in his life. Without a male figure in his life

Your life becomes a living hell. He will have questions you can't answer. Some because he thinks that he is a man, and he will not ask you. Others because he feels that you are his Mom and he just can't talk to you about these things." Mom, how come I wake up in the morning with a hard on? "Mom, this girl trying to give me some, what do I do?" just a few reasons why a man child will not, will not share these thoughts with you as a woman.

Schauntte Parker

And Swallow The Silence

Always there is distance.

Between my mother   and me.

Inside the distance is silence.

Words we do not speak.

Things we learn to swallow.

Sitting in the   backseat of   the Pontiac

orange with   silver fishtails.   Some of the words

come out anyway.

"Remember the time   Daddy   hurt you?"

The silence   between us.   Fills up   like a balloon.

Taking   up   all   the   space   in   the   car.

My mother   looks   through the rearview   mirror.

I shrivel up.

Raisin like.

She swallows me whole.

I am in the kitchen.   Waiting for breakfast.

          A baby is crying.   No. No.   My mother is crying.

                    She is making baby noises.

She has a puffy mouth.   Full of red bubbles.   The hand

around her neck. Is my father's.

I want to hide.   Crawl   under the table.   My feet

          won't move.   Ohh...Ohh...Ohh!   I see.   I see

her head   break.   Blood   on the floor.

                    I shrivel up

          so small.   Nobody notices me.

Mother   spits me out.   Like a watermelon seed.

          "You talk too much.   Be quiet!"

More words are tickling my throat.   I   cover   my mouth.

          Mother has chicken eyes.   Tiny and mean.   Like the chicken

in Yellow Girl's yard.   She   mother said.   "Get me some

          fresh   chicken eggs."   I find a nest.   Hidden.

In some bushes. Got 2 warm eggs in my hands.

Out of nowhere it comes. A chicken squawking. squawking.

Wings slapping. Chicken beak chicken feet

in my face. I drop the eggs. It chases me round and

round the yard. I'm scared so I cry.

"Mommy!" "Mommy!" "Mommy!" "Mommy!"

I can't see her. Too many feathers.
I hear her. Laughing! Laughing at me.

A word wiggles out my mouth.

"Mommy?"

I don't see her hand.

I feel the blow.

See the stars.

Oh the stars.

And swallow the silence.

Lola Rainey

Parenting with a Purpose

By Denise St Patrick-Bell, PhD

A Teenager's Plea

Oh Mother why don't you know me?

In your womb, our two hearts once beat as one united. Then, you knew my every move, felt my every emotion, and listened to hear the call of my spirit.

The Creator, my Creator, allowed two people to become one flesh and breathe the breath of life that became me. Even before I was fashioned in your womb, the Creator already knew me, fashioned me, ordained me, and anointed me to fulfill my purpose.

You dreamed of the day that I would enter the world and now I am here... searching, wondering, experimenting while growing in wisdom and stature. The Creator selected you, Mother, to see me, hear me, guide me, understand me, and love me.

So Mother, the one who knows me best, won't you help me to discover my gifts, my talents, and guide me to my purpose?

In Proverbs 22:6, the Bible says: "Train up a child in the *way* "he" should go, and even when he is old he will not depart from it." For some this is a familiar scripture, but one that is often only aligned with discipline? Training children *in the way they should go* has always been a huge and vital task in every generation because of all that is involved in the process of nurturing children; but has there ever been a time when the challenge was greater than it is today?

When you first hold your newborn, the future and its possibilities flash through your mind. Will he or she be a doctor, an educator, an artist, an inventor, or even the President of the United States? The possibilities are endless. You want your child to fulfill every bit of his/her unique purpose in life. But as life happens, well intentioned moms and dads often struggle just to keep everyone fed, clothed and safe.

From the knowledge of Scripture, child development theory, and from an observation of our children, we know certain things about their *"way"*. First, we know that the Creator has a plan, a course for each child to follow—an orbit for him or her. Second, we know that every child has a specific make up as an individual with certain abilities, talents, and tendencies—a particular bent. Each child and ultimately the adult, is a product of both nature and nurture.

In Educational Psychology, *Nature* refers to heredity, the influence of inherited characteristics on personality, physical growth, intellectual growth and social interaction. *Nurture* refers to the influence of the environment on all of those same things and includes parenting styles, physical surroundings, economic factors, and anything that can have an influence on the development that does not come from within the child.

Research has demonstrated clearly that as a child develops in vitro, learning begins, the educational process is initiated. What happens in the classroom, even in pre-school, is building on what has taken place in the child's life since inception. Effective parenting is key, vital, to educational and lifelong success. Parents often hear that they are partners in the education of their child. That is true. But more than partners, I believe that they are the pillars, the foundation, the critical support beam.

Sociocultural theorists emphasize the role of social interaction and children's cultural heritage in directing the course of cognitive development. Parents are especially instrumental in that they pass along culturally prescribed ways of thinking and responding. As children gain practice in certain behaviors and cognitive processes within the context of social interactions, they gradually adopt and adapt these behaviors and processes as their own. In other words, what they see, hear, and experience influences how they think and behave, and how they learn, play and interact with the world and themselves. How they think will determine how they believe…how they believe will determine how they'll act… how they act (take action) will determine what they'll receive… and what they receive will determine how they live. And it all has its foundation first, in how they consider themselves (*as we think in our hearts*). And that first reflection of self-consideration, the beginning of self-knowledge and self-esteem is based on what is mirrored in the eyes of the parent, the guardian, and the initial caretakers. Children, no matter how difficult parenting may be at times, are gifts directly from the Creator. Whether you are a biological, adoptive or foster parent, you have been chosen to help your child to be all that was preordained for him or her to be.

The voyage of the discovery of self leads to an understanding of our purpose here. Mark Twain is credited with saying "The two most important days of your life are 1. the day you were born, and 2. the day you find out why." Each of us is the composite of our five dimension of Self:

1. The Intellectual me
2. The Physical me
3. The Emotional me
4. The Social me
5. The Spiritual me

A parent's primary role is to create the environment, with willing partners in the child's milieu where he or she can meet and explore each of his or her dimensions.

How can you help your child to live a purpose driven life even at a young age? The environment can foster or inhibit our knowledge of our purpose. But purpose never dies. There are many key questions to continually explore as they grow. They include questions such as: What are the gifts and talents that have been deposited? What type of environment will best nurture those gifts and talents? What role is your child to play in this life? Who does the child idolize and why? Why activities do they initiate without adult guidance? What do they value most? What makes them smile and brings them joy? What do they say they want to do? Often adults fail to listen to the hearts and minds of young children.

What is my purpose?" is probably the most important and empowering question you or your child will ever ask in this lifetime. So help them uncover their talents, their strengths, their values, and their passion. Help them experience new things and develop a plan – any plan, even if it is just a first step. Find ways for them to live life with intent. *And when he/she is old they will not depart from it.* I am convinced that if more young children knew their purpose, they'd have fewer struggles in the teen years. They'd feel a sense of meaning; they'd know where they are headed and concentrate on getting there. Of course dear parents, grandparents, and guardians, as a life-long educator, I cannot leave you without a homework assignment.

1. Complete this sentence: When I look at my child I see …….
2. Make a list of the things and activities that interest your children and those in which they excel.

3. Your child can also ask themselves, "What's the one thing that I do better than others?" This can clue them in to their purpose. <u>Have this conversation with your child. Make it a priority this week.</u> Have you observed your children objectively? For instance, do they like to talk a lot? My friend Dee is a renowned motivational speaker. She often tells the story of how growing up members of her family would pay her to "just shut up." Or are they great listeners? When I was young, children and adults would just come by and tell me all their problems and I listened. Fast forward to my graduate degree in mental health counseling. Are they skilled at building things, or are they good with people? Is their talent more emotional, cerebral or more physical? Together you and other family members can have discussions and talk about the things and activities that interest them and those in which they excel.

4. Make a commitment statement regarding what you will do this week, this month and/or this year to help your child understand the importance of a purpose filled life.

5. Get more information about Multiple Intelligence Theory and the tests, which can expose gifts your child may have but are being overlooked because of our American preoccupation with what is traditionally thought of as being smart.

Humanity is both a mosaic and a puzzle. We each have a unique piece to contribute. That is our purpose in this life. A life that is not purpose-driven is not only self-betrayal, but a betrayal to our collective humanity.

It is Expected of Parents

It is expected that parents will be required to tell a child not wander, ill-prepared, into the rain or the cold...that it is better to act intelligent than merely be bold...to learn from elders and role-models by listening to what is being told...that not every "bill-of-goods" others seek to sell is worthy of being sold...such advice has served young people, throughout the world, since time untold...mentoring in a manner to create an entity that is mature, informed,/ /and/ /from/ /a/ /success-leaning/ /mold./ ./ /.However, by adulthood, individuals should be aware...that there are personal behaviors and actions requiring extra-special vigilance and care...like not reacting to or responding in anger to important political issues, matters, and concerns...to avoid allowing emotional fortitude to determined decisions leading to "crash and burn"...or, to place themselves within the confines of an ocean traveling rickety boat...Which is why it is important that people most likely to be harmed make the best decision when they vote...

King E Carter

Junior Baby's Magic Deacons
Excerpt of a novel by Peter J. Harris
COPYRIGHT ©2016

Junior Baby's Magic Deacons is a comic fable about a cranky, philosophical, old Black man who drives his spiritually souped-up Packard through time and dimensions to round up the four men whose gifts he needs to save the earth from extraterrestrials called Eulipians, who are bent on enslaving human kind based on a terrible secret they've discovered about us. Along the way, Junior Baby teaches manhood, personal integrity, and family history to his primary Deacon, Little Mel September, the headstrong, young son of Junior Baby's best friend from Powhatan, Virginia. Junior Baby is a Black Everyman who 'tells' my first book, *Hand Me My Griot Clothes: The Autobiography of Junior Baby*, which won the Oakland PEN Josephine Miles Award for Multicultural Literature in 1993. Junior Baby's voice is secular, with a spirituality, morality, and metaphysics that bleed beyond his Christian upbringing. He bends tenses, time and dimensions through a souped-up diction and unflappable fearlessness in the face of social injustice, interpersonal drama, inevitable rites of passage, even vampires and hoodoo practitioners who gamble using his integrity as collateral. In this excerpt, the Eulipian mission has ended successfully, Junior Baby has returned his other Deacons to their homes, and has made a detour to share a last bit of history with Little Mel. Pjh

... Now you talking! This why we here in my country crib: Me and Little Mel laughing loudly and deeply, the noise we making putting all them crickets and night time critters to shame. This what I promise to the boy's father! To help his son know why he sang and what real singing is for, how it drag you down into the swamps inside you, or lift you into the visions inside you. How you can't never *volunteer* to keep your mouth closed, not and expect to live a true life and be ready for true love.

We sober up and silently check out the rest of the photos and paintings on the wall. We looking at a country boy, Little Mel Senior, full of good dirt. Working man. Laughter in the lines of his face. Plenty Home Training, but mischievous and always ready for adventure. But a man with a weakness for pretty women and a hankering for scandal. Wasn't enough he have power to talk Plantain Williamson, the love of his life, out her wheelchair. Wasn't enough she the blessing given him by the Almighty. Wasn't enough he love to play the harp of her hairy legs like he promised her. Wasn't even enough she was pregnant when he *Temptation-walked* into the troubles that took him on out and kept him from living in the life of this here boy.

"I sure would have liked to been raised by him Junior Baby...," Little Mel say. "What really happened to him?"

I can't mince no words neither. Can't sugarcoat the story. Have to tell it with all the Five and Dime words I can coax out my memory. I owe it to Little Mel Junior and I owe it to the best in my first Be There Man. Not the weak man. Not the man, whose cheating go against the grain of our friendship. Not the man, who wilt in the hard light of the challenge he need to pass, if he was ever *really* going to *be there*.

Nope, I owe it to the man who I love like my own flesh and blood. I owe truth up in this house to the man whose soul I bargained for to save this youngin standing right in front of me. He standing right in front of me with the biggest need on his face I ever seen. I take a deep breath and exhale one of the stories I was born to tell:

"Messed around with Sophia Shalamar Ragland, that's what really happened," I say. "You may not like this story, son, but I'm duty-bound to tell it like it *T-i-is!* You might not like your father, neither, after what you hear, so stop me if your heart start breaking. I hope, though, to tell it — pus and all — until you get the understanding you need to put all your ghosts to rest, and, who knows, to even put mine to rest, too."

In the silence of my pause, Little Mel don't flinch none. Just stare at me and I know he giving me permission to speak the bitter with the sweet.

"Got his nose opened so wide he swore up and down Sophia put a hex on his ass. Oh yeah, she drove him crazy for sure. But a hex? I'll leave that up to you to figure. One thing for sure is I told him over and over:

'Boy you know the power of the Word, you know the power of Love. God done gave you all the sign you will ever need. Gave you the breath of *healing* Negro, gave you the lilt in your voice allow you to heal the best woman you ever known. Gave you the Rhythm and the Word, the twinkle in your eye, and the sugar in your speech lift that woman right up out of her constriction, right on the dance floor, and right dead into your hungry arms and gallivanting life.' I tell him. I sure tell him.

"Oh but his roving eye and his hungry soul was a bad bad combination. Didn't even have the decency to hook up with somebody outside our little village. Give in to all the raw edges inside him, trembled for the smooth young skin, the velvet promise, the rolling eyes and lipstick hips of Miss Thang, until he not even bothering to make up lies to your mother. Even with her carrying you inside her belly — Lord and I hate to have to lay it down so *hard* son! — he sniffing round the other side of town with this woman. And believe me, the other side of town aint nothing but two, three big city blocks away, if I put it in the way a city boy like yourself can picture it all.

"So, my my my, he might as well been bringing that fast woman home and stashing her in the front room of the home he done made with your mother, the wonderful Miss Plantain Williamson. Well, I can't say nothing right here except in the end he leave your mother, pregnant and everything. I never been so ashamed. Love him then, like I love him now, like I love you now, but it heartbreaking and embarrassing.

"In them days, we all gather round Plantain, men and women, making sure she don't break back down, give in to heartbreak so deep make her lose her locomotion. We all make sure she eat right and think right, so she stay healthy, keep you safe and sound, and hold on to as much peace of mind as we all could help her save. She have only about eight weeks left before you was suppose to make your appearance.

"After about a month passed, we get her situated, and it's clear she have what it take to keep standing. Me, I light out after Little Mel. Like I say, aint hard to find him. We all know where Sophia live. Believe it or not, he stand his ground right in front my face. Tell me he never happier. But even after just a month, I see he *way* out his depth. Bad a man as he is, full of courage in so many situations, he aint nothing now that Sophia done touch him with all her power.

"Beauty? No doubt about that — Sophia put a man's *fantasy* to shame. And her gift of visions — which make her face shine like she opening her ear to a whisper from the Almighty — have him swearing *she* his hearthrob, *she* the bona fide one.

"And, mind you, he done also been *shackled* by her gift of silences in between heartbeat and conversation. You got to understand: Sophia *shout in a whisper*. Speak? She *breathe.* Buddy, she like a silhouette no matter the light, and your father lose himself in the shadow she *don't* cast. She a master in every room of her three-room house, whipping him every which way but loose. Got so Little Mel Senior don't speak so much as moan. Don't walk so much as shuffle. Don't laugh no more, except some fake little cartoon stutter. She hex him alright, but only with what look like to your father a magic promise of a lifetime of irresponsible pleasure.

"See, your daddy a man who live for the eternity that exist in every second. He *believe,* see, he believe with the fever of somebody got faith in the impossible, and he know he *seen* the impossible in your lovely mother who stand up cause she too believe, she too burn. But your Pops, he cocky, think he own the flame, think the flame his number one trump card that he can play at any time. Country boy to the bone, you see, a one-note philosopher. Looking me in the face, *me* who done seen him naked as the day we was born. Looking at me with lies making him cockeyed. He staring two inches to the right of my face, standing in a crack of the screen door, glancing back at Sophia, talking about he staying put, when it's plain he aint even with us on this earth, let alone on the 20 acres he and Plantain Williamson receive as his other gift from impossibility.

"I leave but I keep coming back trying to talk sense to him. I keep coming back trying to represent the one link to *his* magic."

I slow down my story to check in with Little Mel, who breathing hard, touched till his heartbeat got the buttons on his shirt pulsating. But he listening with his whole body, giving me the high sign to keep on keeping on with the words he need to fill his biggest need. I plunge back into the river:

"Naturally, Sophia get tired of having a puppy dog and not a man. She leave. Smooth and quiet as always. Break him right down all the way. All the way. Wildness swallow him up then. Going back home to Plantain Williamson and your newborn self out the question. Sophia move out of Powhatan, Virginia — think she went to Chicago — but I can't tell Little Mel Senior nothing. Son, he on all fours sniffing the house she abandon. Aw, this a classic shame. Finally, after Sophia been gone about two months, I come back and find him ball up in a corner, shaking with the spasm, a puddle of the man he once was.

"But like I say, we take care of our own. I carry him over to see Wilber's Mother Matriarch the power and magic woman, Miss Sovereign Calhoun. Brave her home, which a shotgun house perched on a foundation of mismatched rocks and stones. Only the constant breeze blowing around her home — like it's a swirling Ace bandage — keep that collection of wood and nails and a slate roof from tumbling off its foundation. When you walk up to Miss Sovereign Calhoun's house you must be a bold soul or one so desperate nothing to do but brave the menagerie of possibilities that haunt her location, because believe me, you know *something* going to happen, whether or not it's exactly the outcome you wishing for.

"Her windows painted over in a coat of mango thick enough to keep busy bodies from peeking in, but thin enough so she can see outside. Aint lock the first on the front and back doors, cause nobody sane or crazy enough to try and enter her crib without the clearest invitation from the woman. Period. We may be country folk, who love to drop in on a neighbor when we get so inclined, but 'ner one of us felt free to just up and pay a social call to Miss Sovereign Calhoun.

"And it ain't like she evil or such as that. She help all who come to her in genuine need. It's just that she keep house in such a, shall we say, unique and personal style — sort of like *Conjure Chic* — that she don't cotton to no whole lot of lollygagging. She a *business* woman, pure and simple. And you have to mean business when you step to her with your problem, wish or worry.

"And I'm *serious* that evening I drag your father up to her front door, knock hard, and stand there without breathing and waiting for her to appear. When she come to see who knock, her hair more wild than usual, she breathing fast, eyes and nose flaring. She stare at us like we blow into life straight out the swirl of one of them breezes moaning in the background. She look at Little Mel Senior, throw up her hands and suck her teeth. Boy broke down that bad. Shake her head and look over her shoulder like she missing something behind the curtain separating her workroom up front from the private spaces in the back. I hear giggling of a man and woman in the back rooms and it hit me that beside the crisis your daddy in now, I may have put the brake on some of Miss Calhoun's, uh, personal meditations and recreations, if you get my drift.

"For a minute, I start to tell her I'm sorry if I'm interrupting and maybe if she got time for a quickie, you know, a fixing session where she chain up one or two of Little Mel's demons and straighten his spine for at least a few days until we come back for a full out healing session. But then your father start shaking against my shoulder like he got electricity shooting through his body, and oh God, I forget all about that one-day-at-a-time prescription. Next thing I know, I beg her, plain and simple. Right there on her rickety porch. Drop words out my mouth so heavy they should splinter the wooden planks where we stand.

"I beg that woman in the name of friendship, in the name of community, in the name of the old ways of neighbors. Please help me save my friend. I beg till I'm hoarse, all the while giving your daddy the evil eye to keep him still. Once or twice, I have to snatch him by the collar to calm him down. In the end, I even have to pimp slap him a couple times to let him know we have reach the bottom of the barrel and I am the master and he my slave — that I'm fed up with his simple self.

"Well, Miss Sovereign Calhoun, no matter what other fires burning within her, she see how deep my love is for my brother and she finally agree to work on the boy. She say wait here. She disappear through the curtain and I hear her and the woman and the man all laugh, and she say 'I know I know, but *this* job could take all night' before she walk back into the front room. She come back through the fabric, and I see the folk she talking to tip toeing out the back door, half dressed and just as rumpled as Miss Calhoun when she come to the front door. If I have a mind to comment, the look Miss Calhoun give me bring out the Helen Keller in me, let me tell you.

"Matter of fact, she all the way serious now and waste no time. Tell me to step away from Little Mel Senior. I hesitate but she the best, let me tell you, the best, and aint scared in the least. She fix him with a look let him know she mean business and for that moment your daddy, crazy as he is, know better than to act out. Then she turn to me. She say:

'Sad story this is, I can tell, and for true you asking me to put a hold on my own indulgences, and in this case I was truly ready to indulge.'

She close her eyes with regret and a shiver I feel up and down *my* spine, hmmm hmmm.

'But this *is* my chosen work, and the work for which I've been chosen' she say, 'and I'm duty-bound. I promise you whatever is meant for this boy will come through me. But I go no further without a promise from you.'

"And I tell you son I aint never hear such quiet in my life. Even them breezes cradling her home seem to pause. I know nothing ever going to be the same after I give my word. I ask her what she want from me. She say:

'When this child is healed, when I help him close his circle, you promise to accept it as his bargain with the Forces That Guide. Regardless of what look right or fair or sacred to you. Promise?'

"I sure get a chill but I sure make that promise. Then she say:

'As your payment I want you to make a visit for me.'

"Well that sound easy enough, especially considering how low my Dow Jones is, you know. Originally, I figure it's going to cost me some long green for her to lay hands on your father, bad as he doing. Still, it's sounding all too easy. After all, Little Mel Senior starting to tremble like his skin itching him from the inside out. Eyes rolling and he whispering *Sophia Sophia Sophia Sophia* over and over again. It's ugly and the paint on a moldy masterpiece starting to run, let me tell you.

"I mean it sound simple enough: yeah, agree to make a visit, but aint no way shape or form it's a simple trip I am scheduling. Yet and still, if it save my friend from the worst of himself, if it mean that I can run the roads with my main man again, then aint no extra burden I won't shoulder. Shivering with doubt, my look give her the high sign. She fill in the rest of the gaps. She say:

'There's a gentleman, shall we say, who is also in The Life, with whom I have a ... spiritual disagreement. We have tried between us to settle our differences, but it has become clear to me that it will take some outside mediation, or, at the very least, someone else to take him my final offer of compromise. Promise?'

"A growl from Little Mel Senior seal my answer. I turn and his face twisted with rage and hunger and ache and decay and I barely see the man I love. I'm way beyond shock, although come to think of it Miss Sovereign Calhoun smooth as patent leather. She aint paying no never mind to Little Mel Senior. I'm about ready to explode. I agree, I shout. I agree. Whatever you want, just help him. She smile and turn smoothly toward your daddy, who looking like Pubic Enemy Number 1 and ready to take charge the whole Top Ten list. She take his face with both her hands and the grip strong enough to break his neck, I swear for God, but it also tender as a mother holding her new-born baby. Calm Little Mel Senior right down. Me too, truth be told. Get right quiet in her crooked little cottage.

"He breathing. I'm breathing. She start humming. She hum to match his breath, like she singing harmony. Simple, magnetic, until after about what seem like a hour (but I swear I don't know *how* long the three of us stand breathing and creating serenity up in that place), she step away from Little Mel Senior and walk over to a china cabinet hold brown bottles of all shapes and sizes. She still humming. Me and him still breathing in synch. She pull down one of the bottles, a pretty chocolate-colored thing, with a long neck and a thin line of lavender paint follow the grain of the neck until it coil around the base of the bottle, like a rattlesnake. She pull the cork out the bottle and a fragrance like a mixture of baby oil and rose water fill the room. Get me to thinking of home, of peace of mind. Must have touch Little Mel Senior in the same way because suddenly he smile a distant little thin grin just this side of a look of pain.

"Miss Sovereign Calhoun walk back toward her patient, smell getting stronger, only now it shift — smell like sheets drying in the sun on a clothes line, mixed with grease popping in a pan full of crying catfish. I groan like I'm a child and Little Mel Senior rocking in place, his smile softer. She stand in front of him. Raise the bottle over his head and tip it like she ready to pour over his head all the fragrances it contain. She stop before anything pour out and I stop breathing and Little Mel Senior stop rocking. His face blank in expectation, and that's when she turn the bottle upside down. Only one drop, one itty bitty drop of liquid, fall on the crown of his matted head.

"As she turn over the bottle, she begin singing a lullaby. Sweetest little kindness I ever heard, then or since. She sing to the infant inside that grown man, all the while circling that empty perfume bottle over his head. Aint nothing more dripping from that bottle, but believe me, she *pouring* perfume. I'm getting whiffs of more familiar smells, each bringing images of comfort that soothe me and, evidently, your father, until, unmph unmph unmph, he start crying. Standing right there, shame melting, he break down, and Wilber's mother singing, raising her volume ever so slightly so she heard above his sobbing. His crying and her singing two different sounds at first. A grown man crying and a grown woman singing. But as his sorrow seep to his toes, to the level where his crying reek of the humiliation he feel after leaving his beloved Plantain Williamson, their two voices blend into a larger lullaby that pull Little Mel Senior up on his toes until his head touch the mouth of the brown bottle.

"Listen here, then Wilber's mother start crying and Little Mel Senior begin to croon 'Papa's gonna buy you a diamond ring.' His eyes clear and tears well up in his eyes like they being pumped by a juke joint drummer chewing on three-day old fatback. Finally, he look away from Wilber's mother and stare right into my eyes. He stop singing. He smile a silent, heart-breaking apology at me. He say:

'Look out for my baby.'

"I say:

'No no no, that will be your job.'

"The healing woman pull the bottle from over his head. She still got on her game face, mind you. She *know* it aint over. But me, I'm just happy to see the real face of my Be There Man, and I am bout ready to ask her for directions so I can make my visit as I agree to do. She call his name in a whisper so low I still don't know if she speak for real or telepathically. Once. Twice. Three times. Until Little Mel Senior turn toward her, his face soft but blank, body wrinkle-free, but taut. She say:

'Young man, I know you hurting. I know you overwhelmed with guilt. I know you also mean, got a streak of ugly competition inside you. You must come to agreement with that mean streak. Now, with your own self open as the mouth of this here bottle, each second feel like a new day full of forgiveness. But you and I both know I got to close this bottle and put it back up on the shelf. You and I both know you got to keep yourself open on your own, else no matter what courage you have, what beauty you want to honor, aint destined to be nothing but a quick minute in the scheme of things before you close right back up again, before you give in again to the side that never cries.'

"With that, she hold the cork in her left hand and the bottle in her right hand. In that pause, the old Little Mel Senior still clear cross his face. Confidence. Kindness. Silliness.

Adventure. But then come back fear and the shakes and he whisper *Sophia Sophia Sophia Sophia* over and over again and he stare at Wilber's mama, who don't look like Sophia for nothing in this world. I see threat rise up in him. I see he aint choosing freedom. He aint choosing peace of mind. He aint battling at all. He weak. He don't see who I see. He see the man I found in the corner of Sophia's abandoned house. And he see Miss Sovereign Calhoun as his enemy.

"Well ... right then, I know she break the spell on Little Mel Senior, alright. She done it, which all any healer can really do for his sickness: guide him to the place in his mind where aint nothing to do but to do it — *decide* to be a grown up who handle his particulars, and who know he can't have his cake and eat it too ....

"She lead him right where he supposed to be, the place of understanding we all come to. That place where we understand without no doubt that for the rest of our lives we just going to have to make one choice after another, no matter how tired we get, how boring it all get. As long as we alive, we have to understand, deep down inside, that life simple, really. Everyday, we face the opportunities to fulfill our fantasies, but every fantasy come with its own custom-made nightmare. The trick to balance the electricity that come with the *oh my god* of a fantasy with the gloom that swirl in the *hurricane* of a nightmare.

"Miss Sovereign Calhoun offer Little Mel Senior the power to fill her bottle with his own mix of both fantasy and nightmare. But she know this house call is about over and done with. With a deep sigh, she cork the bottle and hand it to me. The glass hot but cooling so fast I don't have to flinch.

"Well sir, Little Mel Senior make his choice: he jump on her for *healing* him. Now aint that a bitch: get so in love with sickness you don't even want to get well no more.... Anyhow, like I told Wilber up at that gang fight, his mother aint studying none of that from a bruised man acting like a crippled-thinking adolescent. He aint have a chance. It happen so fast I still struggle with whether I see what I see or if I see what I see, you know.

"She *change* his ass! Right then and there. Same hands cradle his pounding head and crack open his spirit now stop him cold with a palm on his forehead, which make him throw back his head and shoot out his chest. She pound the palm of her other hand flat in the center of his chest and lift him about a foot off the ground, where she suspend him to let him know, for the last time, she not putting up with his evil. Then she put him down and he melt until he crouch on all fours. She say, low as when she call his name and give him the choice, only this time he aint got no choice:

'Be wild? Be wild. *Buck wild!*'

"The bottle explode in my hand. I close my eyes to keep glass from cutting my sight. When I open my eyes, Little Mel Senior — or at least he wearing the rags of the clothes he wore when I bring him to be treated — running through the open front door and off into the woods. What I see running not your father no more. But I have come to believe he in the only form that mean his survival, since he choose his fears and wrongs and cold blood over the body of a man satisfied with love, partnership, and passion.

"But just as he disappearing, I hear his voice again. At first, I think it's them breezes kicking up outside Miss Sovereign Calhoun's domicile, but no, I hear the voice of a daddy pleading again, pleading from the place fast evaporating out his spirit:

'*Take care my baby.*'

"I hear your daddy's voice asking his best friend for a forgiveness that counteract any poison I might transfer over to an innocent newborn. I hear your daddy's voice asking me to show you, no matter how long it took, show you, his baby, that he aint all evil, he more than just a Rolling Stone. I hear your daddy's last words *as your daddy* and aint nothing to it but to do it and give my word. Aint no vow but one that bind me to you, son, bind me to a life that lead right here, no matter how far and wide it cause me to travel otherwise. Aint nothing but a simple yes can come out my mouth, his request choke me up so full. This aint no time for *I told you so* or anger or feeling like his selfishness betray me. Only time for this man to be a Be There Man, which boil down to closing the circle between us only way I can at that moment. Only time for friendship to *mesmerize* me, only time to know if friendship either is or it aint. Whatever his body look like, however he remade by the momentous goings-on I have witness, the voice of my *friend* ask me for help and my friend I answer. I answer with my life.

"Aint never see him again, although, I swear, sometimes, I hear him lying Plantain Williamson out that wheelchair, or singing in the trees. You get your voice natural for sure Junior. You may not been raised by him but he live inside you. And that's enough to break the spell them Lipians put on our people."

I point to the open door.

"Come on out to the porch son. Rock a spell with me."

On my porch, I take a deep breath of cricket-filled Virginia night air. Little Mel stand beside the chairs. He sit when I ease into one of the rockers. Hound dog get up and walk cross the wooden porch. He nuzzle up under Little Mel's hand hanging alongside the chair. Little Mel look down at the dog and smile.

"*You* ain't nothing but a hound dog...." Little Mel say with a chuckle.

Sadness sit on the porch with us. Fullness, too. After holding in that story all these seasons, I feel lighter than I have in years. Want to whoop out in joy, but really aint no call for me say one more word. Funny thing, though, I finally find a way to shut him up, only now, aint no sound I wish to hear more than Little Mel's voice. His voice full of questions. His own tales about what he miss out on, what goodness he feel for his mother, who pass on within three years after the turn of Little Mel Senior. His voice full of the new understanding my telling help him gain.

I want it cut and dried, I admit. Want my burden to lift for telling a son his daddy a hero *and* a villain. But no, Little Mel aint having none of the blabber mouth and I can't do nothing but sit and rock, surrounded by his meditation riffing on the silence of the country night, the porch light trembling in the presence of a sky full of starlight.

"And what you know, I blink first. The one man responsible for rounding up the Magical Deacons, for saving the world, *he* the one get nervous. He the one break the silence with one final piece of the whole story.

"I got one more secret for you boy," I say.

Little Mel keep rocking in silence.

Arch his eyebrow just enough to show some curiosity.

And give me permission — and confidence — I need.

Smalltalk with My Six Year-Old Daughter

—When I grow up, your mom is going to die?

—Yes, my baby,

she's pretty old. She will die.

Maybe before you grow up.

—When it's your birthday you'll see her?

—I doubt it.

—Do you want to see her?

—*Of course I want to see her. But she's in California and we are in Michigan*

and we're pretty poor so we can't see her right now.

—You should see your mom, even if she's dead. Make certain

to sing her happy birthday when you see your mom.

David Marquard

Post-Partum Black & Blue

Sweet, baby Sophia, you weaned yourself from my milk early.

        There is no contentment. When you suckle. Only pain.
    Nipples. Left raw. Bloody.

At night, your chirping keeps me awake. Mouth open, tongue quivering.
You demand. More. The formula constipates. Makes you writhe in my arms.

While fat, happy, babies sleep.

        Brown sugar mammy. Bubbling. Sizzling. In the heat.
    Of constant want. Dreams smolder. Turn to ash.

The three hermanas tell me you are teething. They furrow their brows. Suck their teeth saying "¡Probecita probecita!" in sympathy for you.

Maybe me, too.

        A cold clothe. Soothes. Swollen gums. Knick my fingers.
    On razor blades tips. Poking through.

Sweet, Sophia, I want to make you laugh. Humm…mmm you a whale song.
But a frozen scream. Glistens. Through my eyes. Turns softness hard.

Mutes my voice.

        Need to shed my skin. Bones. Crawl inside. Mama's womb.
    Pluck out deadness. Plant a green seed. Let it grow.

Emptiness is a yawning mouth. Full of pointed resentments. Some sharp enough to hurt you. I watch you scoot across the floor. Dragging one foot behind.

Like a wounded animal.
        Wild creatures. Gnaw off legs to escape. Captivity. Here. Take.
My tooth. I must flee. This house. And you.

Lola Rainey

Illustration by Joe Geran: Spirits of the Wind

mariachi plaza adjacent

Santa Cecilia, music's patron saint

Caridad del Cobre, lady of the sweet salt waters

pavement meets horizon

to see beyond the spotty mirror

visions drive sunset

mirror of a mirror empañado

refraction imborrable

espejo enterrado

a firearm's rear sight

smudged

mirar para adelante es mirar átras

tras las dudas

doubts are lenses

lance the eyes

at times the heart

fall back

spring forward

en medio winter

frozen in humidity

en lo indecible

sweat beaded at 100 degrees overhead

indelible words sketched in ears unheard

unsayable

unreadable

in the palm of the hand unsaid

released to the waters from clasped hands

copper shimmers undulating

vision frozen with red light at intersection

points west as the sun sets from the east

filtered lenses

backbeat

que fue

lo que la vida es

fractions of what was

visiones

what life is

Gloria Enedina Alvarez
2016

HEARTS OF SAPPHIRE

by Emory Holmes II

"The sapphire is a precious stone and is blue in color most like to heaven in fair weather and clear, and is best among precious stones and most apt and able t fingers of kings."
— Bartholomew Angelicus
(13th century)

"Set me as a seal upon thine heart, as a seal upon thine arm: for love is strong as death; jealousy is cruel as the grave: the coals thereof are coals of fire, which hath a most vehement flame."
— Song of Songs VIII: 6

The great Cumberland River was blue, deep blue when poppa dove down to it and struck it and flashed inside it but what momma liked most about the Cumberland was not its edges of blue which showed in the shallows but the black depths showing in the center of its great rushing currents where it trembled dark blue and shimmering. It was those dark blue depths, which poppa entered gladly, that she loved.

Momma stood out on the bank of the Cumberland and sang. She sang a song to poppa. Poppa whose song flashed inside her. "And he was blue, dark blue like the water, son," she said.

And that's what momma sang about at the bend on the edge of the Cumberland River. And that's what she taught me to sing, too, and play on the horn. Though she told me many stories they all were linked like the story of her father running away from the Civil War and hiding rather than kill someone or be killed by Americans and of how his courage was a different kind of courage than the courage of the white folk, that it was the courage of a conviction not to die rather than the courage of a conviction to die for them, for their causes which he only felt as a horror which caused him to flee and to hide amongst the Indians where he met his wife and loved her and made momma with her. An Indian. A half-red half black girl who sang like a wonder. A girl in whose voice all her days were reflected: the treachery and languor of the South, the glamor of Harlem, the splendor of Siam.

When poppa first came into town everybody thought he was a Dandy. He was black as a boot and shining and had a mean laugh and when he looked at you he looked right though you. In most of the stories momma told of him poppa just appeared one day. It was his blackness that made her look at him. Momma said when you saw poppa's blackness it made you shiver like you were seeing something suddenly. Poppa and his brothers were musicians and he played the cornet like no one else.

In some of her stories poppa was just a boy and a champion swimmer. She depicted him out in the Cumberland with the water rushing down and his face flashing blue against the white of it. She'd show the black boy flashing down the current of the turbulent waters and the Cumberland laughing and playing over him like a muscular serpent on the back of a manchild. And momma would sing, "Yes that was him, boy," she'd sing, "that was your grandpoppa. Him swimming out there in the water, black as a beet and pretty."

Then she would point and bring the whole scene to life. She'd make a sweep of her beautiful hand and you could make out all of Nashville with the great blue Cumberland swimming into the gesture. She showed the big city brimming with movement and folks displayed about it in the attitudes of toys. At the core of each of her stories, whether their outcomes were tragic or lighthearted, was the fathomless depths of some dark natural thing whether it was poppa's eyes or his blackness or the swirling depths of the sky or the Cumberland or the deep interiors of her wedding ring's stone winking on its bed of diamonds or poppa's dark jealousy or the fathomless depths of her own heart, laughing in darkness, all were blue, deep blue. And at the end of each of her fables, momma stood out on the blue edge of the moment, her arms thrown out and singing.

Those were the days when she was a little girl in a little town called Trinity, Alabama. When she did the girlish things and was in love in little ways with little boys — the *beaus* she called them — one by one, multicolored, cinnamon and red and black and gingersnap colored. How they danced and played ball and the big barns loomed over them when they kissed and the moon rolled blue over the flaming redness of Alabama and sank in the deep blue body of the night. "And that was a part of the sapphire, son," she said. "That was part of the bigness of it when you finally saw what it really was and that it was all around you and not just in the little places — the little hard nuts of wonder." And she showed me the ring.

This, too, was her heart of sapphire.

She would thrust her long red fingers into the light and the ring would flash once, twice. Her strong red fingers were long and graceful like an artist's. They were long like vines of sugarcane or curving avenues of brown and red earth or ribbons of some sweet and wonderful thing. Those were my grandmomma's hands. Momma's hands.

The crown of her material possessions was the sapphire wedding ring. And that was a nut of memory no one could rob from her. She played the Royal Circus of Siam with poppa in 1921. Thousands of spectators sat out on the grass of the royal grounds and listened. Afterwards the king sent a man to poppa. When the man held out his hand it was enclosed in a glove of black velvet laden with a fist of beautiful stones, some of them rubies, some of them diamonds, all of them precious. He thrust out the black velvet glove to poppa and said, "Take Sir. Take what you want of the stones."

And poppa smiled and looked at momma. "You choose, Baby," he said and momma, just a girl then, fifteen or so, she grinned and looked down at the stones and then up at poppa and down again and that's when she saw the sapphire, chilling the others with its brilliance and singing down in the center of its crude blue heart. She plucked out the stone and thrust it into the light. To her, it was a heart. A live heart. And she gave it to poppa. "It's for you, Daddy. It's for you," she said.

And poppa smiled and took her in his arms.

And that was a good story. And that was one way she told it. Of how she got the stone. And poppa told it other ways. How the sapphire was actually birthed in the head of a snake he was training and decided to kill. Cooly, he had bust the snarling head open and drew out the stone and turned it over to momma and said, "Baby, this is a heart. This is the heart of the snake. This is the snake that stole the love out of Eden. This is the snake that bit Eve and when he bit her he chilled her with the blueness of his heart and the blood in his mouth burst in his head like a star."

Yes this was the star poppa stole and gave back to momma. This was the way that poppa said it (or sang it) or played it brightly on his horn. And no one ever heard such wonderful playing. And no one ever saw such a blue and wonderful jewel.

Poppa had it mounted on a band of white gold and set in a starburst of diamond baguettes — this was his heart of sapphire and he gave it to momma. "Don't never love no one but me, Baby," he said.

The lamplight struck his face with a shock of green when he gave it and he repeated the curious sentence, "...not even the beauty of the stone," he added with finality.

He looked at his Love, and then at the ring. It flashed once, twice. They returned in the spring and the New York papers ran a photograph of them arriving. Some of the photographs were tinted blue where they showed the priceless stone from Siam. A Nashville paper ran a tinted photo of momma up on the bandstand and the stone flashing with its turbulent brilliance.

"Your grandpoppa was just a boy then, son," momma would caution. "He was jealous and mean but he was a peerless musician."

Whenever someone would talk to momma poppa would rush up and say in his deep voice, "What's happening, Baby? What's going on?" and flash his wild jealous eyes.

Momma would laugh and tease poppa for being so evil but sometimes there was nothing to tease and there was only his violence to contend with. Poppa with his pride and toughness and swaggering manner had made many enemies and was jealous of all of them. He suspected them as momma's suitors.

The two men he hated most were most like him. One of them, Sonny Boy, was a criminal and big as a barn and black as a boot and pretty and was sweet on momma. He played the horn, too, though not as fine as poppa and drove a bootleg truck for the white folks at night from Nashville to Cincinnati. He was a man from the underworld.

Poppa's other rival was a man from Tuskegee who had gone to college and who talked so sweetly and earnestly about marvelous things and about momma that momma loved him secretly like a girl loves a dashing man in a daydream. One day the man from Tuskegee took momma's hand into his own and whispered to her his story of the sapphire.

"The sapphire," he said, "*was a piece of deep blue Heaven broke off by God and made into an angel. The angel was bid to watch over Eve in the Garden lest she be tempted; but the bold angel fell in love with the Evening and ran away to love her. So it was that Eve fell into temptation and Eve and Adam were cast out of Paradise. God raged and changed the angel into a star and hurled him out of Heaven. The angel struck the earth and shattered into a thousand blue stones stamped with the tale of his love with the Night and showing in each heart the fire of Heaven.*"

The man looked at momma and drew her hand to his lips.

He smiled, "*Each of the stones contains its star revealing the tale of Eden. When anger is kindled in the heart of the bearer both desire and rage burst forth and tremble its heart.*"

The man said this with a flourish and kissed momma's hand. This was his story of the Heart of Sapphire.

And that was a good story, too, and maybe that's why poppa hated it when he heard about it. He hated it for being a good story concerning the woman he loved. Its message struck him and he cried out like a beast and lurched into the pit of the night, his eyes flaming.

When he returned he was changed, both aimless and frightened, his clothes gashed open and dripping with blood. "Pack your stuff, Baby. We got to go," he croaked.

"What's wrong, Poppa?" momma asked in terror.

"I killed a tom cat," he muttered darkly.

"But we —."

"Don't question me woman!" he cried.

They argued for an hour then poppa ruminated and rang up his enemy Sonny Boy and they struck up a bargain and poppa slammed down the phone. He grabbed momma's hand and they fled into the night out to the great forests beneath them that fringed the rushing Cumberland. She cleaned his wounds in the Cumberland and they hid in the shadows in the rushes until evening, trembling and gasping like animals. At midnight Sonny Boy arrived in a truck. Poppa scrambled out of the thickets and the two men loomed black in the moonlight. Then Sonny Boy let out a big curse and shouted, "Pay me, boy. Pay me now or I'll sell you to the goddamn paddy rollers."

He laughed like a big bear when poppa trembled.

Poppa said, "We ain't got no money. I told you I would get it to you soon as we reach Cincinnati."

Sonny Boy laughed in poppa's face and grinned. "Pay me," he purred and pulled out a pistol.

It flashed in the moonlight. Momma walked out of the rushes and put her arms around poppa. He would not look into her eyes but she grabbed his face hard and looked into their depths. What she saw made her knees wobble. Poppa's eyes were white with fear and emptiness. All of this goodness, all of his strength, all of his wildness, all of his sweetness, all of his prettiness had trembled out of him. The light rushed out of his heart and into her eyes and shimmered in the moonlight; they flashed once, twice. She turned to Sonny Boy and drew off the stone. "Here," she said. "This will pay for it."

And that's how momma lost poppa. He was gone for good that time. He turned around and his heart failed him and he could not look at momma but simply leapt in the back of the truck amongst the bags of contraband Sonny Boy was hauling. Sonny Boy took the stone and laughed and covered up Poppa and drove off. And that was the month that momma birthed my daddy. In a decade she married Sonny Boy and that's how grand poppa came back to her. He came back in the form of the stone.

CODA

Poppa Nightingale (1895 -1930)

Momma (1905 - 1976)

Poppa's sound was full and complex and moody. It was stacked up and blue and sweating like the Alabama woods he grew up in. There he and his brothers ran like wild deer over the sweating wasteland through the dark mists that rose blue and feathered the moor. The boys came out of it black leaping like deer.

When poppa played his horn the notes shimmered like bullets ripping through brass, confronting something deep within the heart of the song and shattering it. When poppa sang with his horn the notes were special and individually wrapped and went out with a kind of joyous and bright virtuosity that made each one in his audience a solitary listener.

Poppa stood out in the street playing his strange, joyous music with his brothers and jeering at the passersby who would not listen. He was at the center of them, momma said, his horn sparkling and raking the air, him dark blue amongst his black olive-faced brothers. His face was shiny and hard and his eyes flashed like the eyes of a great resting animal. They were the eyes, she said, of a stallion, or of a great flashing river.

Whenever momma told me a story about poppa she would repeat the individual parts of it over and over until I could play them on the horn. I saw the life that shimmered just beneath the words and saw their mists coming up over the Cumberland.

Sometimes the mists she made with her words were pale blue like that of the dusk or the morning and when the mists of her words rolled back there lay the fathomless depths of their meanings shining in the waters beneath them and showing a flashing star of laughter deep in their centers. This was what she put into a song to make it heartbreaking and wordless like a movement in nature. It was something, she said, she got from poppa. Then she'd look at me and say, "Now you play it, boy. You show me the story back on the horn."

And I would play it back to her as she had sung it. I would try to make the music spare and unsentimental and make it punch the notes and shatter them like she said poppa could do with his playing when he was most savage and most simple. I would show him in the voice of my trumpet and try and put all of his travels into my phrasing. And at the end of each movement I would show my grand momma standing in the blue of the moonlight her arms uplifted, her throat quivering, her heart dancing and racing with the song going out of her and piercing the vast blue depths of the night.

Checkers

by Mark Thomson

One jump, two jumps, three jumps, king me

Old and worn, the squares begin to fade

The checkerboard, gathering dust in a corner

It could have been my grandfather's

A faint touch of hair tonic rides the breeze

Mingled with stale cigar smoke and echoes

They greet you at the door, smiling

Reminders of another time, they beckon

Tuffs of gray and white, sprinkled about the floor

Caught by the gentle breeze, they dance

Across the black and white linoleum

A private ballet without the broom to lead

Where are the men who once filled these chairs

Who will tell their stories, so often repeated

Who will teach young men life's virtues

Patience, appreciation, respect for the passage of time

The strap has fallen into disrepair

No razors are left to stroke and sharpen

Brittle and cracked, it hangs beside an empty chair

Waiting, hopelessly, to be brought back to life

The brush is no longer flexible and soft

Long ago the dance across a rough face ended

The mug now filled with cobwebs

Will warm suds ever fill it again

These aging tools, what fine teachers they were

Trapped in a day when the sun measured time's passage

Before man and machine together removed

The virtues of slow and steady patience

One jump, two jumps, three jumps, king me

Old and worn, the squares begin to fade

The checkerboard, gathering dust in a corner

Will it ever be mine

The Passersby

by Erica K. B.

<u>5:56 PM</u>

The fresh rays of sun were slicing through a smog of gray clouds, finally ending what had been a long set of rainy days for Harlem, New York. As if ready for the weekend herself, Mother Nature was done with the Renaissance, deciding it was time for the states of the Deep South to enjoy what she had in store for this year's hurricane season. She spent quite a time in Harlem, making good noise with the rest of the jazz creatives. Beating down rhythmically on avenues and boulevards of row houses and tenements. Four days straight, just about. The sun would now shine on the city for the weekend, and most of that summer 1932.

As the glow of that evening's sun flickered into a rugged tenement window, the bittersweet feeling of ecstasy was fading from the bedroom of 22 year old Davis Day. The self-driven bandleader worked hard and romanced harder. Especially when the lady was as iconic a beauty as his one-time fiancée, Alma Walton. The spitfire mulatto woman traced her hands over his bare chest, wondering where the essence of their love making had gone. Perhaps it was moving on, with the rain. It was the story of their romance. One minute she loved him, the next she could not.

The electric Davis had only courted Alma a year before asking for her hand in marriage. Two weeks later, she put that engagement ring back in his hand. All to end up on his box spring three months later. Funny how things changed, much like the seasons. Davis grinned, noticing the moods playing out on her ivory face. Her hazel eyes bouncing from her thighs to her hands, and suddenly on him.

"Yes ma'am?" he said so huskily she lost her breath.

Alma blinked away from him, taken aback. She snatched a pillow from behind him and laid down on the squeaky box spring. Careful not to get to close, but close enough that they were touching.

"Nothin'. I'm just thinking."

"What about?"

Alma's eyes rolled, landing on the slightly open window with a not so promising view of laundry lines connecting to the tenement beside it.

Davis sighed, frustrated. He could never seem to break through to her. He never did reach a conclusion on what it was about himself that made her unable to love him. It couldn't have been his music. He chuckled to himself at the silly thought that it was. Maybe it was his tacky domain. A run down place to call home, but it was his. And it could've been hers had she just minded her manners and bit her tongue some. He should've known the moment she auditioned to be a show girl that she was a bearcat never to be contained.

The only thing Alma loved was her dreams, and he didn't blame her. He never would. But boy, did it drive him mad. She would never be his, no matter how tightly they embraced in moments of physical expression. Those same expressions maddening him with the thrill of every climax she reached. She was such a lovely work of art, worthy to be admired despite the opposition she stirred.

"Say woman," he began with a tender smack to her thigh. "Where you headed later tonight?"

"The comedy joint with the Italians," she answered without a beat.

"Playing the harlot for that ol' mob boss again?" a slighted Davis asked. He got out of the bed and went for a trumpet in the room's corner.

Alma gasped at his insult. "You mind your manners boy! I ain't no whore."

"Well ain't he giving you money for your time?"

"My time and my lovin are two very different types of company, and I'm not discussing my personal business with the likes of you." Alma pulled her golden hair away from her face as she turned to face him. "Now. What time is your show?"

"We play at midnight. At The Monarch."

"I know where you play."

"Does that mean you're coming?"

Alma grinned, thinking it over. "Reckon I just might." She was now dressing into her dress. She too, like the rain, was moving on with her day.

Davis chuckled at that, staring back at the sparkle in her eye. "I won't hold my breath." He lifted the trumpet to his lips. The vibrant sound it produced rippled from the walls of the unit and echoed out the window, down the tenement walls to the wet floors of the dark alley below.

"You're a wise man." She winked at him and floated out the door. Taking the stairs two at a time, she slapped a felt cloche hat over her pin curls before stepping out into the streets. She hurried down the avenues of Harlem, smirking at the whistles and cat calls she often enjoyed ignoring.

"That there is a pretty lil white lady, ain't she?" said a young black boy, beating a set of pots and pans on the steps of a brownstone.

The boys older brother, charged with watching him make his noise, retorted, "Alma Walton her name. She real friendly round these parts in Harlem..."

She almost slowed her strut to eavesdrop longer. But Alma continued on to the brownstone she shared with her mother. It had been far from a quaint upbringing in Harlem. She almost wished her mother had just given her up to an orphanage. Instead, she endured a wretched and lonely childhood as the mixed race daughter of a mother who she could not relate to, and father she would never know.

It was a life muddled with insults from the black mother she caused much grief, as she was a constant reminder of the shame of a cold evening in Richmond, Virginia - 1912. Winnie Walton didn't make it home from work early enough, and she paid very dearly for that when cornered by a group of white boys in Church Hill. One of those boys had a very sterile lust, and in the midst of his turn of rape, he had fathered a pretty little baby girl who would forever be stained with his golden brown hair and ivory skin. Uniquely set apart from the woes that plagued many African American communities, but forever entangled in the struggle as the daughter of a black woman.

Tensions between mother and daughter had reached new degrees when Winnie migrated north in 1925, seeking to escape the racial tensions dominating the Richmond area. The final straw being the lynching of her fiancé. Those white devils had taken everything from her, including her right to a pure black first born child. She saw strength in those blacks who said to hell with the south! Her days of walking on grounds drenched with the blood of her generation's past were over.

Alma remembered riding a train out the Main Street station, with Winnie's instructions of "don't ever look back." Winnie heavily involved herself in work as 12 year old Alma began what would be a very hard journey of fending for self. She would no longer have the comfort of Grandma Sallie to hold her close to a warm fleshy bosom, scolding her youngest daughter on her inability to love her baby.

She would say, "Winnie you gots a mighty fine price to pay with God for not lovin this child. She ain't no curse like you sayin. Why all babies is a blessin! Your Uncle Harry- believe it or not, him the son of our mama's master. She ain't hate him like so..."

But those were times that felt ages ago. Grandma Sallie had went on to be in glory with the same God she said would hold Winnie accountable. Alma had grown into her insecurity, with a resolve that focused on her dreams of stardom and addiction to the bright lights of New York City. She had ripped loose from the claws of a traumatic childhood, finding satisfaction in her liberties as a white woman in Harlem's wild nightlife.

Alma could hear her mother's cackle as she turned the key to the door of their home. She braced herself, wondering what spectrum Winnie was on at the moment. She had been drinking far more heavily in the recent months, and even took up some light prostitution if it meant the habit would be supported. Both john and bottle were accompanying Winnie this late evening, and Alma hoped to get as quickly as she could to her room without an insult from her mother.

"Who's that?" the john asked, making sure Winnie didn't see the lust formed in his eyes at the sight of Alma.

Winnie lifted the green bottle of moonshine to her full lips, narrowing her eyes at Alma as she turned a key into her bedroom door. "She ain't nothin special. C'mon baby. Let's do it again." She ran her smooth hands over his shoulders as Bessie Smith's croons sparked the fire that was her desire to love him. It almost cooled when she saw the concern that hid itself in his eyes when Alma slammed the door to her room.

Alma rushed to her vanity and ruffled through the contents of her drawers until she clutched something- anything she could throw at the wall. Anything to release the emotions of anger she felt from simply walking into the home. The jar didn't shatter, but the top had broken off and the creamy contents were all over the carpet.

Realizing what she had thrown, Alma hurried to the floor and scooped the bleaching cream into her hands. It might've stained the carpet had she not gathered all she could, and rubbed it onto her face. Smoothing the cream over every part of her face and neck. She would've bathed in this stuff if it meant removing every trace of black in her blood. Those European immigrant women did it all the time. Played down their more ethnic features and gussy up the white standards of their beauty.

It would be only a few short years before Alma planned to dye her hair blonde and relocate to the golden shores of California, in the hopes of being a grand TV star. Her current life of passing and escorting in Harlem would soon pass away. She would be free to live life as the pure white woman of Hollywood high society.

Alma's day dream was fading with the tingling of her skin, letting her know the cream was working. Right on time. Pepe Pasciano hated when she was running late. She would be awaiting his arrival in just another thirty minutes.

10:45 PM

Lora Dee Gilliam was knockout beauty, and most of Harlem's nighttime was going to find out. Those who had yet to encounter big round eyes so docile were prone to ponder the secrets of the ornate soul housed within them. She was unlike any of the colored doll faces that paraded the night clubs, dancing with the glee that made life worth living. Her southern charm stood out amongst the brash attitudes of women of the north, especially those seeking to pave their own way in society.

Yes, Lora Dee had the ability to tingle the blood of any gentleman she decided to engage in conversation. She embodied the mystery of woman that kept the world populating- with a body that cleaved to its innocent virginity while bursting at the seams of womanhood with attractive curves at the bosom, waist and hips. Skin as deep as the night, and as mysterious as the southern folklore taught to her by her mother while her father served in World War I.

The newly 18 year old was a bunny to the world of Harlem when she first arrived from the Midwest town of Orberlin. It was the town flood of this June that gave her the strength to hi-tail it to the grand city. The northern winter had been harsh to her, especially as she made earnings as a dishwasher in Little Italy. That was where she found favor amongst the flattery of the Italian men that enjoyed her type of bold beauty.

Mob boss Luigi Mariano asked her to work as his maid in his penthouse, on the upper west side of Manhattan. He could barely speak comprehendible English to her, his words becoming littered with eh's and ah's as he concentrated hard on how to phrase his affections.

"I'm a-so sorry bella. But eh, you are a-one of the most bellisima donnas I have-eh seen ever. In-ah this country. Make a-me a most happy man. Be my help, my maid. Si?"

Luigi would pay a fine price of ten dollars a week, which was a fine wage for a single gal in the city. On this afternoon, Luigi had ask her to accompany him to the comedy club he and his buddies often frequented after hours.

"Be your date to a comedy show? Sir Mariano, would your wife approve?"

Luigi grinned, and stumbled over the words, "Mi a-wife is old. She a-don't like the nightlife like-eh I do. She do not a-bring me the joy your smile a-bring me. She knows this. Understand?"

Lora Dee's cheeks warmed as she pondered the excitement this scene would bring her. "Oh fine! What time must I be ready?"

Luigi kissed her hand and said, "I will a-get you promptly atta 9:30."

And he was prompt in his arrival. His jaw practically dropped to the curb when Lora Dee stepped out of the Harlem tenement. Her chocolate skin swaddled in a tin silver fringe and beaded dress. For something that fit so loosely on most of the modern women of the time, the gown clung to her figure - highlighting the curves that very clearly said to men she was a woman. A beaded feathered headband was fashionably perched on top of her finger waves.

"Pretty neat for a moll, right?" she giggled, striking a pose underneath the streetlight. "Let's put on a ritz!"

"You are ah the thing the dreams of my fathers are a-made of!" How badly Luigi wished she could be his lady. He kept his arm tightly around her as they traveled a few boulevards down to The Orchid Theatre, where the comedy show was taking place.

Their authentic smiles baffled many of his partners, and the wives, girlfriends or escorts thereof. Particularly Pepe Pasciano and his date, Alma.

"Who's that colored woman on the arm of Mariano?" she asked with a tug of his sleeve as the black beauty and mob boss entered the theatre room.

The ogle Luigi gave when turning his eyes on Lora Dee rattled his date. Although, she would never let that be known. Alma cleared her throat in an attempt to gain his attention.

"I don't know her," said the fast talking Pepe. "You?"

"Why would I know her?" Alma lit a cigarette and blew its smoke towards the large chandelier rounding at the ceiling's center. "Are they sitting with us?"

"Of course. Now you can get to know all about her." Pepe raised his hand and beckoned for Luigi's attention.

Within a few moments, Alma was watching the mob boss pull out the chair beside her for his date. The lady sat down, and smiled at them.

"How do you do?" She looked on lovingly as Luigi introduced her to Pepe in fluent Italian. Pepe perked up at the sound of her name from his boss's lips.

"Why it's nice to meet a colored woman of your beauty. A complete doll, she is!" Pepe shook her hand with such enthusiasm, one would've thought she was a celebrity or model. "D'ya smoke?" He offered her a cigarette.

Lora Dee put a hand up, refusing his offer. "No, thank you Pepe."

Alma stumped his foot under the table. "Ya gonna introduce me or what?"

"Lora Dee, this is my date, Alma," Pepe began. He looked Alma right in the eyes when saying. "The woman you asked me about earlier is named Lora Dee."

Alma blew an angry puff of smoke in his face. "Yes Pepe, I am aware." She turned to face her. "We've never caught the boss out with a date. Nice to meet you. From Harlem?"

"Oh no. Me? I'm from a little old town in Ohio."

"The Midwest!" Alma feigned an interest. "How long ago did ya arrive?"

"Been about a year now. Don't get out much though. Can't say I know from nothing what it's all about."

Alma grinned at this bit of information. "Oh my. Why you're amongst some real owls, you know? The nightlife in Harlem is what bring people from all over the world here. It can be real overwhelming to a sap that ain't ready for the whoopee of it all."

Lora Dee thought that over. "I can see that. Guess that's why I was little shy about escorting Sir Mariano tonight."

"He's a real egg, ain't he?" Alma asked, seeing that Luigi and Pepe had struck up Italian conversations with other mob members. "Where'd he find a dame like you?"

"I'm his maid."

Alma nodded, figuring it so. "Oh of course."

"Where'd you meet Pepe?"

Alma took a puff of her cig before indulging Lora Dee in details of her relationship with Pepe. "He saw me dance at a show, couple months ago. Waited for me backstage, took me to dinner, got a crush on me... Next thing I know, he and I were going to these comedy shows every week. A fair exchange of company and affection for a little dough. Nothing wrong with that, right?"

Lora Dee hoped her face didn't hint at her disdain. Nevertheless, there was something magical about Alma that she admired.

She continued, "Oh I can't just beat my gums about me all night. Tell me more about you. Who are your parents? Where are they from?"

"Back in Oberlin, Ohio. My mama was a seamstress, and my daddy served in the war. I don't know why. All he done did was come home a very dreary man. He don't even believe black folks can have American pride."

"You don't say!" Alma guffawed.

Lora Dee shrugged her perfectly sculpted shoulders, bearing an expression of relaxed hope that showed she felt otherwise. "Why, nothing make me happier than the thought of what I can become in this here country. That's why I came to New York. I just know it's better for me out here. I ain't gon be no body's maid forever."

She paused only a short breath before looking deep into the hazel eyes of Alma Walton, asking, "So what do you do?"

The white woman looked back at her, and while there was a wonder, it certainly wasn't with the same splendor Lora Dee hoped for. In fact, Alma couldn't help but wonder why this young lady reminded her so much of her mother. Except her deep cocoa smile was much more inviting. Posture straight, hands open, eyes wide with excitement and a voice that delighted with a songbird pitch. She was everything Winnie was when she wasn't interacting with her daughter.

Alma blinked away a welling of a tear. And that scared her. No one had ever moved her spirit like the eyes of this here Lora Dee. She ashed her cig, and did so rather coolly.

"I dance."

"Oh my, do tell!"

"It started as ballet. Nowadays, I like to swing it with the big boys at the juice joints. The Monarch, in particular. You ever been?"

Lora Dee dropped her jaw. "Oh no. But it sounds like the cat's meow!"

"Oh it is, darling!" Alma assured her.

"Seems like you live a mighty exciting life!"

Alma shrugged, sporting a naughty grin that showed she agreed.

"-I mean for a white lady and all."

Almost choking on her smoke, Alma reached for her glass of water on the table. "Pardon me."

Lora Dee appeared remorseful. "I didn't mean to offend. I mean, we black folk hear so much about y'all... sometimes it's mostly bad, but it sho is nice to meet some friendly white folk like ya'self. You're a real flapper, I'm sure. Exciting! I'm glad I came."

"Oh stop!" Alma was surprisingly bashful. A part of her yearned to reveal she was half black. The last person who made her feel that way was told that secret, and Alma paid very heavily for it. The admission of true self would always require a reflection of the people and problems that made her strong, only after they broke her down.

For the first time, Alma was allowing herself to enjoy a woman's company instead of rivaling in it. "How'd you like to high tail it outta here and over to the Monarch for the midnight show? After this?"

Lora Dee nodded very gleefully. "Sounds like a nifty idea!"

12:32 AM

The band jolted with the pump of every horn as swing dancers energized and entertained seated guests. A pianist bounced his shoulders as his fingers slammed hard on the black and white keys producing a quick pace blues melody. A bass player tapped his foot and thumped at the strings of his large instrument. He nodded his head with every thump, as if one with the instrument. A clarinet player closed his eyes as he breathed life into a sound that was a perfect balance to the other instruments.

The electric spirit of swing was grabbing a hold of various guests. Some downright tossed their handkerchiefs to the table and got a wiggle going onto the dance floor. Davis fed off this energy.

"Yeah! Baby's casting a kitten on the dance floor, ain't she? Doggone good! Let's take it up a notch Duprees!" Davis said to his band.

The drummer led the way, rumbling the cymbals and snare into a quick high tempo beat. Worthy of all the vocal scatting it would ensue from Davis. The others got with the fast flow and began a lovely tune that showcased the best of the dancer's quick and happy feet.

In the club's rear, Alma and Lora Dee entered the joyful event. Lora Dee starry eyed, and Alma composed.

She grabbed Lora Dee's hand, saying, "C'mon! I got a table up front."

She hurried her to the table for two near the stage that had a perfect angle of the band stage and dance floor. It was lighted by a candlestick wedged tightly into its holder. Two glasses of water were immediately brought to them.

"Do you dance?"

"Nah. I'm a dead hoofer."

"Lora Dee! Don't be such a flat tire! You must get out there with me tonight."

"Oh no, I insist…"

"And so do I!" Alma hoped her genuine smile eased Lora Dee's anxiety. She could smell it radiating from her pores the moment she asked if she danced.

Davis looked around the room. It was filling with guest, all hear to see him and his band play some of the best music on this side of 125th. He lifted the mic to his lips, roaring,

"Baby just leavin the hen coop,

Gettin ready just for the night-

Baby just left the hen coop,

And she tell me everything's alright-

Baby just left the hen coop,

And she barely got time for romance –

Baby just left the hen coop,

And all she wanna do is dance."

Davis winked, rhythmically slapping his hand against his suit and swinging his baton toward the band. He bounced his eyebrows while charismatically looking around the room. Particularly for the fresh faces of women in the crowd. There were a couple of regulars. A few new Janes.

"*Wellllllll* look at what we have here…" Davis shrieked into the mic.

"Oh doggone it." Alma blushed as she and Davis made eye contact. While she certainly wished she could high step it on the floor, she was off duty tonight.

He grinned, speaking, "Look who we have with us tonight. Alma! Who that pretty little dame there with ya?" He danced toward their table, and held the mic towards Lora Dee's lips. "What's your name baby?"

Alma was unnerved in her seat. Embarrassed. She certainly thought Davis was coming to her. This was a much unexpected admiration.

"Lora Dee." Her smile was hard and dazzling.

"You look like a singer. Are you a singer miss lady?"

Lora Dee clapped her hands with joy, laughing brilliantly as she answered, "Oh my! Why yes I am! I love to sing."

Davis held a smile as he turned to Alma. "You been givin this lady some of that giggle water or what?"

The crowd chuckled. Alma rolled her eyes at him. "Oh get on with it, Davis."

"You say you can sing Miss Lora Dee?"

Lora Dee stood up, proud. "Just you give me that mic. I'll show you."

The crowd roared with approval as Davis led her by the hand towards the front of the stage.
He became weak in the knees as he stared into her eyes, handing her the mic.

"Sweet baby," he whispered to himself. He shook himself out of the daze and faced his band. "Let's keep it up tempo, shall we?"

Lora Dee caught the beat right away, adding her own twist of jazzy lyrics combined with bluesy scatting that was met with cheers and applauses. Her alto groans careened into a songbird falsetto of high notes that jolted the spine of those dancing.

"Lay it on em baby!" Davis cheered on from the side, waging that baton at the band. "C'mon boys. We got us a live one! We're hittin on all sixes!"

Alma looked on at the scene Lora Dee's had brought to life. As if this young gal couldn't get any more special, now she can sing her heart out! Alma lit a cigarette with the flame of the candlestick. She watched with deceitful fascination as Davis and Lora Dee exchanged scats. Something inside her burned with the slight spark of jealousy. But the prideful Alma would best conceal it until she could sort through its muddled feelings, and later deem them anything but envy.

"Give a round to Miss Lora Dee!" Davis said to the crowd.

The cheered and called to her as she made her way back to the seat.

"Quite the voice you got there…" Alma said, forcing a grin.

Lora Dee giggled, "Makes up for my two left feet."

3:38 AM

Francie's Diner was always jumping with the late night crowd, especially after the shows at The Monarch and other Harlem clubs. Francie made sure to serve the hottest combination plates of dinner and breakfast. Often chicken with waffles or pancakes. Grits, sausage, bacon as well. She even kept a fresh tray of mac and cheese ready for the early AM rush.

The stuffy diner was crowded with guys and gals who had just enjoyed a night of music, dancing, and prohibition. Now they were crammed inside a tiny diner, hands flapping for a waitress's attention.

Amongst them, Davis Day and his Duprees – Flo the pianist, Gus the bass player, and Ed, Reggie and Slap of the horns trio. Alma and Lora Dee were with them, being pressed into smoky suits as new guest squeezed inside.

"Everybody just wait a damn minute!" Francie said, waddling across the kitchen with two hot plates on her arm. She served two guests, and called for a waitress. "Mabel! You get ova here now! You see this crowd!"

Mabel hurried in from the back, fixing the hair net on her head. "Ok, who was first?"

She was greeted by a host of "I was" with the waving hands to match.

"Oh Davis! Do we have to eat here? Can't we grab something elsewhere?" complained Alma. She was shoved into the back of Reggie. "Sorry Reg."

"Lora Dee ain't gone get no better chicken and waffles than here at Francie's. I say we wait it out. What about you, band?"

The men agreed. Alma sucked her teeth and folded her arms across her chest. Lora Dee noticed her sulking.

"We don't have to stay Alma. If you want to get out of here, let's go!"

Davis wasn't too fond of this suggestion. "No, Lora Dee. Just give it a few minutes. We'll be eating soon!" He stretched his arm high, calling out, "Francie! Francie! Got you no room upstairs? We hungry, ya hear?"

Francie marched right up to the Davis Day and took him by the nose with her two fingers. "You watch yo mouth boy. Or I'll make sure the only thing you conduct is your manners towards women." She released him to a host of laughter.

"Real funny Auntie."

"Boy you see all these people. Calm yo'self." Francie pinched his cheek lovingly. "Besides, upstairs is full. You gone have to wait. In the meantime what'll ya have?"

Davis placed a round of orders, and within thirty minutes, he and his band along with Alma and Lora Dee were in the diner's upper room enjoying their meals.

"How you likin it honey?" Davis asked Lora Dee.

She wiped the crumbs from the side of her mouth, swallowed her grits and answered, "My my. It's simply divine. You be sure to tell that to Miss Francie. Say boys..." She rose from her seat. "Where is the ladies room?"

Flo pointed her in the right direction. When she was out of earshot, Alma leaned over to Davis.

"I know what you're doing. And you can just cut it out. She's new to Harlem and she don't need no trouble from the likes of you. Besides, she's my friend so have some dignity about yourself." Alma started to light her cigarette.

"Alma," said Davis with a song in his voice. "Do I detect a bit of jealousy on your part?"

"Don't be ridiculous. I'm not jealous at all. I'm telling you don't get no funny ideas about that ole Lora Dee." She looked him the eye this time. Maybe he'd take her serious.

"A friend you say?"

"Davis..."

"Just curious."

"We met not too long ago."

"As in a few hours back?" Davis chuckled. "She already told Flo a little bit. What's gotten into you, Alma?"

Alma scuffled from the table, mumbling, "Oh get outta here Day! Move over, Slap!" She wedged herself between the two tables and headed down the stairs.

"Where'd Alma go?" Lora Dee asked. "She turned in for the night?"

"Something like that. C'mon and have a seat doll. One of the fellas will get you home," Davis assured her.

"Ain't she pretty neat for a white lady? We don't see too many forward white folk like her!" Lora Dee was actually excited to rave about her fascination with Alma in their company. "Do y'all know her from dancing?"

"White lady?" Flo snickered. "Boy oh boy, she done got over on you too?"

"I beg your pardon…"

Davis intervened, "Don't mind him. You see Alma is a mulatto. Half white, half black."

Lora Dee was visibly surprised. "She is? Why, she ain't tell me that?"

"Wouldn't expect her too, if she was hoping to pass as white," Flo added. "Tell me this, darling. With pipes likes yours, you looking to get into the music biz any time soon?" He fought to steady his heartbeat when she smiled that knockout smile at him.

<u>4:02 AM</u>

Alma noticed the man on the other side of the street. He too was puffing a cigarette. A small bottle of gin was concealed in his pocket. She could see the bottle's imprint through his slacks. She was just gutsy enough to approach him for a light when her cigarette went out.

"What's a white lady like you doing round these parts of Harlem?" he asked, striking a match for her.

"Same thing a white man like yourself is doing. What joint you coming from?" Alma asked him, sporting a half smile.

He grinned back. "I'm actually a mulatto. Half black. Can you tell? Guess you can say I'm from around here." His green eyes sparked as he pushed his dark brown curls from his forehead. "I stay just two blocks down. What about you?"

Alma looked at him, curiously. "In the brownstones."

"Nice. I'm Harry Scarsdale, by the way." He reached for her hand. "What do they call a beauty like you?"

"Alma… Alma Walton. A pleasure to meet you."

"A pleasure indeed. So what brought you out tonight?" Harry asked. He carefully removed the bottle from his pocket a stole a sip of gin.

"'The Monarch. What about you?"

"Get outta town! I was just there too! First time. And boy, it didn't disappoint. Did you see the honey scatting with the band? Wasn't she great?"

Alma was able to contrive a, "Just peachy."

"Oh boy! She was a knock out. Voice and all. Say, can you sing?"

Alma looked down at her pumps. "No. I'm no singer. I do dance."

Harry's face lit up with the light of excitement. "You dance? Well so do I!"

"Really?" Alma asked. "You swing?"

"I can. But I had a classical upbringing. Mostly tap nowadays. I perform at The Mill in a few days. You ought to see me."

"Maybe I might," Alma replied. "If not there, certainly again sometime soon." She gave him a suggestive look.

Harry hadn't ran across a woman so open with her intentions. A part of him was turned off, while the other liked it very much so. "Perhaps. Say, Miss Walton, how's about I walk you home?"

Alma was so ensnared in his green eyes, she couldn't even answer. She simply grabbed him by the hand and they began to cross the street. At the same time, Lora Dee, Davis and the band members were exiting the diner. Lora Dee spotted the couple first.

"Davis! There she is there! Should we call to her?"

Davis looked at the backs of Alma and Harry, fading down the avenue under the streetlights. He wrapped his arm around Lora Dee and said, "Nah. Alma's a big girl. Let's get you home doll face."

5:06 AM

Harry and Alma never did make it back to the brownstone. They stopped in an alley to exchange hits of reefer. They were giggly, jiving with each other on music, dance and other aspects that connected them to Harlem life.

"So you a half breed eh? Ya mama black?" Alma asked as she nestled her face in the place of his arm pit. The highs of the reefer slowly creeping down her body, from the mouth she inhaled with down to her stomach.

"My mama, actually. A New Yorker born and bred. As progressive as they come she was. So I hear."

"What happened to her?"

"Died in childbirth. And wasn't none of her white family members takin some nigger baby in. Let them tell it, my mama got what she deserved for having a black baby," Harry answered.

Alma shushed him. She a finger up to his lips. "Don't talk like that. That just ain't right."

"I lived twenty three years with this. And this the first time I don't heard somebody tell me not to talk about it. And from a white lady! Get that!" He snickered wildly, almost unable to control himself. "This reefer givin me the heebie-jeebies."

Alma was stone faced and still as she looked at him undergo a fit of giggles. The thing running through her mind was how to tell this man she too was a mulatto. If there was anybody she could reveal the darkest part of herself to, surely it would be someone who had the same mixed blood as she. The difference between them being he had managed to live his life an openly biracial man. She suddenly yearned to know the deeper, more complex parts of him.

"How do you do it?"

"Do what babe?"

"No no! Not that." Alma explained, "Live in society as a mulatto. Do you ever worry you'll face… you know… a harder time… because you're black?"

Harry took her in his hand and started them down the dark alley. He clung to her tightly under the incoming sunlight, answering with, "I don't worry at all. In fact, I've found kinder faces in my black brethren. As opposed to the hidden racism you find in… well, white folk. Ain't as bad in New York as it is in the Bible belt. Whew doggy! Some folk like to think the South won the Civil War. My grandpa and grandma raised me to be a proud black man."

She looked proudly at him. Like a wife would a husband. A mother would an army decorated son. A daughter would to her long missed father. The same tear that Lora Dee has cooked up was forming in her eye. She wiped it away when he turned his head.

"What about you? Your parents from the States? Or some country across the pond?" Harry asked. His fingers tightened themselves between hers. The sunlight was peaking over the two tenement buildings they walked between. He usually was in his the window of his room to watch the light of day brighten. Right now, there was no other place he'd rather be than conversing with the lovely Alma in the streets of the city.

"No. They're good ole American. By way of Boston. My mother moved us to New York when I was twelve."

Harry smiled, exposing his dimpled chin and perfect pearly whites. "And you've been a riot ever since, haven't ya?"

Alma laughed a hearty laugh as they turned onto her street. Recognizing the same streetlight that had welcomed her home many of nights, she cleared her throat. "This is my street. I can take it from here."

Harry would have none of it. "Oh don't be silly. I walked you this far. Mind as well take you all the way."

"No, no. My mother would kill me if she saw me on the block with a colored boy," Alma lied. Harry almost looked sad. She stroked his cheek tenderly and said, "Listen, I had a great early morning with you. Hope it's not the last."

"Come to my show. Please?"

Alma thought for a long pause before saying, "I promise."

Then Harry did the unexpected. He leaned in and kissed her cheek. Alma puckered her lips, awaiting one on the lips. But she could feel him pulling away. She tucked the same embarrassed lips away behind a sheepish grin.

"Have a good day," she cooed. She turned on her heel, and a slight jog down towards the brownstone.

She never saw that Harry had waited.

<u>5:54 AM</u>

Alma turned the key to the door as quietly as she could. Winnie hated to be disturbed this early in the morning. She was probably sleep in the fog of alcohol, reefer and sex. The living room was a disheveled mess. She tiptoed into the kitchen for a drink of water, only to be met by the shadowy figure of someone there. Alma jumped for the light switch, and it was revealed to be Winnie when the light flickered on.

"Oh mama! You scared me." Alma sighed with relief as her hands were brought to her heart.

A loud smack to the face knocked her to the ground. The blow and the pain it caused released a flood of childhood memories of abuse. Only then did Alma realize what had happened. She held her burning cheek, and looked up to see her mother starting for another strike. Alma rolled out of the way, and screamed,

"Mama! What's wrong with you? You drunk woman?"

Winnie pushed Alma towards the bedroom door. She ranted and raved, "Elmer asked about you when we was makin love. What you done did to him? What look you done gave him? You white whore!" Another smack to the other side of her daughter's face. "You white whore! You gave him the eye? Put a root on him!"

"You are mad! You looney old woman! You're mad I say!" Alma defended herself. "I ain't put no nothing on Elmer. You better get yourself another john!"

Winnie reached for a glass from the cabinet and hurled it at Alma. It barely missed her, crashing into the wall above her head.

"Get the hell out!" Winnie screamed, at the top of her lungs. "Get out you whore!"

"Mama! It's me! I would never do that to you!" Alma cried.

Winnie raised her clenched fist. "You get outta here! White devil, out!"

Alma wasted no time in hurrying into her room, locking the door behind her and packing a bag. She grabbed the funds she had been saving up and placed them in the suitcase. She tossed a few set of clothes in the carpetbag and ran out of the home as fast as she could.

Out in the street, the sun was now in the sky, lighting most sides of Harlem. Alma followed the light to the end of the corner, where she saw Harry was hurrying to.

"Harry! Harry!" she called after him.

He hesitated, but then turned around slowly to face her. He would have to admit that he followed her to the door step, and had heard the entire exchange between her and her mother. And for the life of him, he couldn't understand why Alma's mother would refer to her as a white devil.

"Are you alright?" he began.

Alma tossed her bag down on the ground. "Do I look alright?"

"Was your mom… mad… that you came in past curfew or something?" Harry tried to appear as unknowing as he could.

Alma reached into her bag for a cigarette. Harry moved to strike her a light.

She huffed, "No. That damn lunatic accused me of putting the moves on one of her suitors."

Harry nodded, and wondered if she would address the white devil. But what Alma did next seemed like something long overdue. She let out a deep wail, one that started from the pit of her diaphragm. She collapsed to the ground, and buried her face in her hands. The cigarette had rolled off the curb, and into the sewer.

"Alma, Alma, Alma!" Harry rushed to be by her side. "What's wrong girl? Tell me it all."

Alma spent no time thinking it over. The words seemed to have the power to push themselves right out of her mouth. She revealed to Harry, "My mother is a black woman. She hates me. My father was white, but I never knew him. I just know the very thought of him sickens my mother, and she sees his face every time she looks at me. She hates me Harry. She hates me."

Alma almost hoped her mother would hear her agony from the confines of the home. This was a pain long withstanding. The hurt of it all hitting her like a ton of bricks in this very moment.

Harry shushed her, and to some degree that worked.

"I get it baby. I do. And I'm sorry to hear this Alma. I really am." He rocked her back and forth in his arms, hoping the motion would pacify her tears. "Listen, you can stay with me until you get back on your feet. How does that sound?"

Alma calmed herself only long enough to answer, "Yes, thank you kindly."

Harry lifted her to her feet and grabbed her bag in his free hand. He looked into the eyes of Alma and said, "Don't run away from who you are. Her inability to love you is not a reflection on the colored people whose blood you share. You know that right?"

Alma wasn't sure. She could only cleave to his shirt, crying twenty years' worth of sorrows and heartbreak. And in his arms the tears came and fell. As if Mother Nature herself had returned to Harlem to see what all the morning fuss was about.

Cecilia Manguerra Brainard

P.O. Box 5099

Santa Monica, CA 90409

Tel/fax: 310-452-1195

Email: cbrainard@gmail.com

Copyright 2016 by Cecilia Brainard

(Please note my copyright in the publication, thank you)

A Sensorial Mecca

by Mark Thomson

    a rich pot of gumbo

    a newly-lit bowl of sweet honey Cavendish

    fresh baguettes, still hot

    coffee with chicory

like fingers of a flame

unbound by gates or walls

licking around the corners

ignite passions, consuming everything they meet

    the bold, brassy, boast of a trumpet

        young, exciting, new

    the mournful wail of a saxophone

        old, weary, tired

    the rich, mellow voice of a trombone

        deep, full, mature

    the Caribbean mystique of steel drums

        vibrant, alive, dancing

unfettered and free

they leap through the air

carried on the breeze like nature's dancers

tickling the ear

but echoing throughout the soul

    street vendors hawk everything

        hot beignets dusted with powdered sugar

        caricatures in bright pastels

           Mardi Gras beads that will never lose their luster

    old iron balconies filled with honeysuckle vines

    horse-drawn carriages covered with red carnations

    oysters and crawfish

        full of color and ready for lunch

    living bouquets

           welcome and beckon a springtime eternal

           wisteria, creep over an old brick wall

           bougainvillea, spill out from a window box

           banana trees, shadow a patio fountain

a broad collection of colors

compete like little children for attention

the panorama is full, accented by cheerful sunshine

choreographed better than any ballet

What I was supposed to be writing
Excerpt for Itz All In Your Womb

This is NOT the book that I thought I was writing. I am the author of the book Whatz In Your Womb...and in my mind, Whatz In Your Womb is a franchise and I would be following up with my second book called Whatz Your Womb Thinking? Well, that's not what happening. What's happening is that this is about recognizing that it's all in the womb and has always been. This thing is about a being...a being with the awareness of herself or himself as a Soul, God, or Higher Self with a perception that extends to the entire universe and beyond. It's about this mystical organ in the body that led me to understanding my being. Through trying to find out the divine secrets of the black woman's womb, I instead found the divine secrets of the Soul. I found out that I am a soul and I have a body....not the other way around. So now I freed the body of being responsible for carrying and containing the soul which can't be bound. I freed the mind from trying to integrate with a soul bound by the body. Things are now back in natural order. The body is free to be the awesome and flawless unit it was naturally designed to be. It is no longer under the stress of believing it is housing a soul. Think about it; the only time a body houses a soul is during pregnancy and then it releases it after the 9 month. Any mother knows that after a time, you are ready to have your baby because you are not only feeding two bodies, but two personalities, and two souls. After awhile, it feels stressful. Well imagine housing a soul for 40+ years! It's like being pregnant your entire life...how stressful is that? And then, how confusing for the personality who is supposed to translate and integrate the signals from the soul and the body? No wonder why we wander around life aimlessly and constantly searching for ourselves in relationships, organizations, groups, families, lifestyle, books and research, movements, religion, anti-religion, etc? We won't find it because we are already it. We just haven't realized it yet.

Maat em Maakheru Amen

Illustration by Joe Geran: Guardians of the Sea

Only Love

Love is like a flowing river traveling the length of life's reality...

flowing for various lengths of time, from short periods until finality...

There are bottlenecks and speedways, where matters come fast and furiously...

Sometimes, too fast and with such strength that it is difficult for the traveler to see...

There are long and short stretches where the movement is comfortable and smooth...

And there are periods providing the sailors with false sense of solace and soothe...

There are rough spots with waves churning/ dangerous/ and/   /high./ /. /.providing/ /an/ /illusion/ /of/ /a/ transparent impenetrable barrier from water level to the sky...

There are travelers who learn from each repeated experience and step...

And there are those who learn nothing and thus, are in a state of constant wept...

The wisdom is that while young and strong...

Listen and learn that which will make love's journey wonderful ad long...

King E. Carter

Beauty is Not Monolithic

Beauty is not a monolithic reality and concept…

It is diversified, possessing levels and layers that many cannot identify, and that others cannot accept…The physical aspect is most obvious to those possessing only basic sight…The internal-emotional, personality, and behavior-components, however, reveal matters within a greater scope and light…

King Carter

The SS Pacifica

This is an excerpt from the novel, *The Newspaper Widow* (the University of Santo Tomas Press, forthcoming), all rights reserved)

by

Cecilia Manguerra Brainard

It was Samir's mother who had said, "Take Didier and go. I'll be all right."

The idea had germinated, taken root, and like a wild plant branched out and filled Samir's mind. With Melisande's letter in his hands, Samir had read to his son the part about the two talking mynahs in a huge cage beside the picture window with the mannequins.

Didier, who had been his biggest concern, lit up when he heard about the birds. "I can't wait to see them, Papa. Do you think they'll talk to us?"

The boy had not even turned to say goodbye to France when their steamship, the *SS Pacifica*, pulled away from the dock of Marseilles; he was busy studying the seagulls, gannets, and other seabirds. Later he drew pictures of the birds in his sketchbook — Didier also had a passion for drawing.

And so Samir and Didier sailed on the *SS Pacifica*, which traveled at 20 knots per hour, and slowly they left behind the cold European winter. The ship paused at Port Said for coaling, and father and son watched the glowing torches of the barges carrying the coal. They strained to see the shadowy figures hauling heavy baskets up steep planks to the steamship, the men singing in unison while they worked. It took eight hours to get the job done, and by then, the sun beat down on the statue of Ferdinand de Lesseps. Samir's chest expanded as he told Didier of the marvelous feat the Frenchman had done — ten arduous years it had taken de Lesseps to unite the waters of the Mediterranean and the Red Sea; ten years Samir had been separated from Melisande.

Slowly, the *Pacifica* inched through the narrow Suez Canal. At times it seemed the ship would scrape the sides of the canal; and just a stone's throw away was Egypt, with its people, camels, donkeys, and ancient ruins. He bought from some men on feluccas, a silk jalabiya for Melisande and a fez for Didier, which the boy kept on his head even while they dined with the ship's captain and surgeon. (They had peacock and camel's hump for dinner that night.)

Samir sketched the enormous sand dunes that reminded him of his painting of his mother in the Arabian dress, the same image that had upset Melisande, but which drew them close. He often thought of that Sunday, that afternoon of lovemaking — the memory helped sustain his spirit.

It had been with them, Desire, from the moment Melisande had stood outside his apartment door, through lunch, on to the drawing session on his balcony. He had seen a shadow cross her face when she finally saw his drawing of her. It was not unhappiness, she later explained, but all emotions that welled up, that indeed his work had feeling. He had pulled her close and touched her face, slowly as if he were a blind man committing it to memory — his fingers molding her cheeks, her forehead, her eyebrows, her lips, his fingers sliding down to her neck, to her shoulders. He had caught the scent of citrus from her hair. He had desired her, knew he could take her, but restrained himself. Later that afternoon, it was the portrait of his mother that drew tears from her eyes — she had mistaken the Arabian woman for his lover. How could he stop himself from saying, "Spend the afternoon with me. I want to give you pleasure." There was no protest, no resistance as he bent down to kiss her forehead, her eyes, and then her lips. With his hand around her waist, he had led her to his bedroom, and he had cleared away her things from the brass bed, and lifted her unto it.

That day, after they had made love, he told her that Plato said humans were originally created with four arms, four legs, and a head with two faces. But fearing their power, Zeus split them into two separate parts, condemning them to spend their lives in search of their other halves.

He had told her that they were very fortunate they had found each other, because they were meant to be one. He said, when they part, it will hurt them very much, because the one-ness will be separated once again.

They had been apart for years. They had suffered. It was now time for their two halves to become one.

Melisande.

The *Pacifica* chugged on to the Bitter Lakes and then to the Red Sea. By this time, they knew their ship by heart: their first class cabin with its side table always stocked with Turkish delight and other delicacies; the smoking room where Samir chatted with the men; the promenade deck where they walked and gazed out at the ever-changeable sea; the women who fawned over Didier, their eyes sparkling at Samir as well. And there was the library where Didier scoured all the bird books; one afternoon, he appeared wide-eyed in front of his father to report that mynah birds could die from loneliness.

At the southern end of the Red Sea, they stopped at Port Aden where they caught a glimpse of the twin minarets of a mosque, then like a birthing, they passed through its gulf into the Arabian Sea. As he studied the wide expanse of the dark sea, Samir knew with certainty that Europe and the desert sands of Arabia were behind him. His throat had tightened when he considered that Melisande had been in these same waters after she left him — how could he have driven her to this distant place?

Melisande had always been in his thoughts. From the time he and Didier had boarded the train in Paris, he had tried to imagine the voyage she had taken a decade ago. He saw her on the ship's deck, in the dining saloons, the music hall, in all the port stops they made — there Melisande was, tall with her woman's figure and long curly red-brown hair.

Their next stop was Colombo, Ceylon, where they stared in awe at the modern General Post office and grand hotels. During their port stop, he bought a thumb sized sapphire stone, violet-blue in color. That evening, he sketched a ring design for the gemstone, with Melisande in mind.

A few more days at sea and they arrived Penang in Malaysia where he saw an elephant hauling logs near a river. The air was more humid now, and the sun gleamed white, and the sky and sea were brilliant blue, and the palms and birds of paradise startling in their crayola colors.

Then one clear morning, after travelling for 21 days, the *SS Pacifica* made its way through the strait between Mactan and Ubec islands. The captain had warned them of their early morning arrival, but suddenly, Samir and Didier were unprepared, their things scattered in their cabin, Didier's books and toys lost in tight corners.

After packing the last of their belongings into their bags, Samir and Didier left their cabin and hurried toward the boat's railing to stare at the larger island, Ubec, a name they had only read, but which now held their future.

"Papa, are we here?" the boy asked, his voice quivering with excitement. He had on a white sailor suit, crisp and immaculate; it had been buried in the bottom of his suitcase, kept new for today.

"Yes, Didier." Samir held his son's hand tightly.

Samir's bravura had deserted him last night. He had peered out at the velvet darkness of the sky and sea and he had felt drained, afraid: He had left his work, his mother, Paris — his past. Had he done the right thing? Did Melisande have the capacity to forgive him? Would she be able to love this boy who was not hers? With Didier snoring softly near him, he had rummaged for her letter and had reread it for the thousandth time — she loved him still.

Didier swayed from left to right, straining to see more of the sea and the sandy shore with coconut trees and nipa huts; and the boy pointed at the lush green mountains that ran down the center of the island like a spine. Later, Didier's eyes fixed on some boys and girls who were playing in the water. "Papa, look, children." Didier waved at them. "Can I also swim in the sea, like them?" he asked.

"You have to learn to swim first," Samir said.

"I will, and I will also visit those mountains. I am sure there are many birds there, talking ones, like the mynahs." Didier became thoughtful before adding, "I wonder if the mynahs will sound like a phonograph."

Samir mussed the boy's hair; a feeling of well-being surged through him; he had not felt such happiness in a long time. "We'll find out when we're there," Samir said, his voice redolent of hope.

~

The City of Ubec loomed ahead, with its old Spanish fort and plaza, the stone churches, the sparkling white American buildings, and the myriad wood and stone structures that seemed strewn haphazardly. It was early morning in December, and the weather cool for the tropics. Ines closed the door to *The Ubec Daily* and hurried down Cristobal Colon Street toward Printemps. She knocked and opened the door. Melisande's assistants were not yet in and the shop was quiet. A long time ago, before Melisande had moved in, Ines had seen this place. It had looked like a warehouse then, rundown and dirty. Melisande had transformed it into a vibrant dress shop that the women of Ubec loved. The hanging dividers and mirrors gave a sense of space and light, which made visitors feel as if they were walking on air. A beveled glass showcase near the door displayed items that Melisande also sold: crystal bottles of perfume, alabaster pots of skin lotions and makeup, bed linens, tablecloth with matching napkins, lace handkerchiefs. There in the back section were two Singer sewing machines, silent this morning. A large bird cage and two mannequins wearing Melisande's haute couture faced the picture window. Ines hurried up the stairs to find Melisande in her bedroom. She was seated in front of her dresser mirror, studying her image while brushing her thick mass of hair.

"The boat is coming," Ines said, out of breath with excitement. She had in her hands sprigs of jasmine, whose scent filled the room. The jasmine vine outside her bedroom window, had grown back thicker and healthier, filled with cascading clouds of sweet snow-white flowers.

Melisande moaned. "Oh Ines, I've gained two kilos since I last saw him. And my hair is so unruly today … and oh, my skin …" She reached for a pot with rouge which she lightly rubbed into her cheeks, leaving her skin glowing pink. Melisande stared at her image and made a face. "Look at me, Ines. I look terrible."

"There is no time for that now. Felix said the boat is almost at the dock."

Melisande gasped. "And I haven't checked the shop." She quickly anchored her hair into a bun using combs and pins, and put some powder on her face.

"I'll make sure everything is in order." She found a vase, filled it with water, and arranged the spray of jasmine in it.

"But what if he notices that I've … grown old?"

"What does that have to do with their arrival?" Ines asked, perplexed.

The mantel clock chimed just then — it was getting late — and Melisande twirled around, threw her hands up in the air and laughed.

"Go, now!" Ines said.

Melisande picked up her purse and umbrella and she and Ines ran down the stairs. Melisande kissed Ines on the cheeks, blew a kiss at her mynahs who were half-asleep in their cage, then taking a deep breath, opened the front door. She stepped outside and hailed a carriage. "To the pier, hurry!" she told the driver. "I have to meet the *Pacifica*," she added in a voice breathless with longing.

~end~

Our Failure to Say Farewell

Please, I spoke, let's not talk. It's not

a language if we never listen, if we never

fucking understand each other.

Please, I said, again and again:

let's just close our eyes.

Maybe you're right, she said: there really is nothing

left to say.

David Marquard

Pillow Talk

Reach for me. I push away. Swim upstream. Silver scales decorate. The current. Petrified tears. Muddy water woes. Shred my mermaid tail. Bitty pieces. Floating. Nothing left. Below the waist 'Cept brittle bone. No feast for you here.
Gut me anyway.
Pin me down. Suck the scream out my mouth. Rough tongue enters…splinters. Brittle bone pieces. Float by. Us.

Roll off easy. Legs, arms flopping like a hooked fish. Gasping for air. Fix a dark liquid eye on my skeleton fins. Dripping salt water.

You say. Don't wanna rape you. Girl. Wanna make love. Next time.

Lola Rainey

Pornosophy (rev.)

It just appeared: out of the hardening

aperitifs and episodic brain food.

Starving morsels of oiled oleander

and dazzling decayed apparitions.

Stumbling to the ditch of the most rabid

wretched Hell-Horns of Desire. To kiss.

Mating is meeting our own shadows in

The scrupulous sanctions of engorgement.

"Why is it so hard?" she asks. And he zips

his backward Brainchild - the bibulous beast.

Animals! They act like Animals! Beasts!

Watch them rut; rotten relics of The Freeze.

The breeze blows blameless, and harmless is the

Night. Stroking our pointless legs to lather.

Climactic Spectator Sport of Kings and

Oft' time Queens and Jacks: off to see unfurled.

And watching it! Seeing the Budging Bear!

The low-hanging basket of True Passion!

- 2 -

Still hidden from view, the Cosmic Scrotom

Pleads the Fifth, and heaves into view. Show us!

And empties the sacral Ambulance of

Shame's last call. Calling home: "Thank God, it's you."

"It's time for Our Time, our singular slow dance -

Our Eden with crotchless panties; aren't they?"

And tapping the tapeworm's relative ease

On silver screens, the Mouseless Endomorphs.

Stop! Stop! Stop!

But they'll never Stop!

Never put it back in.

Don't want to.

Why should they?

Why indeed.

Martin Perlich

Illustration by Joe Geran: Willie Tucker

The Museum Visit These Many Years Later

And if I were a middle-aged poet
from somewhere northeast
with sand on my shoes, I would say,
Oh! if only I had learned something yet,
standing here in front of you these many years later.
But wisdom is its own burden.
I understand a bit after all, standing here.
It was you, with those wild tips streaming out
like nightchills, like the sun's harbor, like a splay
of penknives from so many deep pockets, sitting in solitude,
in silence, gold covered and gold inside, you dance on,
despite the change in weathers, the politics and styles,
the fears more urgent with retelling. My silence is its own
in this small moment. Shiva, they have moved you here
in temporary display, making my journey back to you
a little mysterious, a little like maya, anyway. And
there you are, dancing,
just like before.

Susan Booker Morris

[This is my first poem since the snow began to fall]

I sat down to drink
my silent cup of tea
and watch the tree out
back
and saw the branches shape
a caucasian man's face
with a cigar between his lips.

It surprised me...
this face with the
snow falling perfectly
through the space where
his eyes and throat
should be...

I hope to see him again
[this spring, perhaps]
when the birds fly
through his tender
smiling face
in the backyard
in the tree
on the branch
which now
belongs
to him.

Phillip B Middleton

Swamp Woman

We meet in a hotel lobby.
Hello. Dark eyes soak me in.
Tight puckered lips part.
Swamp water gushes out. Embarrassed.
She flees. Down a hallway. Leaving muddy
prints. On the carpet.
We meet again. Outside a café.
She floats by. In silver sequins.
Green curls. Adorned with shells.
Billowing in all directions.
Join me. Her "O" shaped mouth. Flattens.
Into a blue-gum-smile.

Over a bowl of seafood. Consommé.
Swamp woman. Tells me her story.

Ah waz born in da biyou. Swamp wata in mah blud.
Lil' whil' back. Ol' hoo' owl com' to mah windo'.
It waz a'bino. Wite. Wit big ol' pink eyes.
Ah dream 'bout snow. Fo' da fers' tim'. Now dat all ah do.
Tink 'bout sno'.

Mah ol' man sez. Som'un' dun hoodoo ya.
Mah auntee. A root woman. She sez naw, gal'.
Ya got a callin'. Gotta stan' in da sno'.
Fin' out wat it be. So ah took off. On mah ol' man's hog.
Gon' to Cado'rado. Up in dem mou'ens. Gonna fin' me som' sno'.

She finishes. Her meal. Then drifts into the night,
Moving slow. Easy. Like muddy water. Flowing.
Into Lake Pontchartrain.

We meet. A final time. In a dream.
Strips of gray skin. Dangle.
From a skeletal frame.

Empty. Eye sockets.
Blaze. White hot.

Patches of mossy green hair.
Hang. Loosely. From her scalp.

The rot of death. Decay.
Is nothing. A mask.
Mardi Gras disguise.
Waiting. To be cast off.
Revealing. A steamy.
Swamp essence.
Immutable. Wild.

Deaf. Waz callin'. Mah nam'.
Dun tuk me way. F'om e'rtin'. Ah luv.
Wanna kep me. In da col'. Gron'.
Cain't be. Too much Lous'ana. In me.
Gonna walk. Dis earf. 'Til' judgemen' day.
Meltin' da ice. Turnin' sno'. Into swamp wata.

Now. When I hear people. Talking about
Icebergs melting. Polar bears drowning.
I see Swamp woman. Flooding the world.
Trying to baptize. Us all. In muddy water.

Lola Rainey

Yesterday's News (Live)

Gray sky
  soon to be blue.

Dark, dead leaves
  soon to turn green.

Yellow moon
   soon to vanish entirely.

Summer-quiet morning
  soon to unfold.

Noise to come
  with engines
   roaring.

Later: darkened eyes,
weary
eyes strained from
too much work.

2/
Yul's message
resonating [I don't care what you do...but don't smoke.]
wearing black, he...

LeRoi's voice

still screaming [the don'ts of this white hell.] screaming

into the avalanche of history and into his son's inner ear.

Tony Rosato running into the blue sea...

[out of my way, you revolutionaries, as you bomb blast Belfast to death!]

3/

And the unenviable retreat and the alarming melancholy that's drifting in from Sarajevo.

Phillip B. Middleton

"Certainly there is no hunting like the hunting of man, and those who have hunted armed men long enough and like it, never really care for anything else thereafter." **–Ernest Hemingway**

The Snapshot

by Pam Ward

An excerpt from the novel, "I'll Get You, My Pretty."

The word 'snapshot' was a hunting term describing a quick shot without careful aim. With the advent of instant photography, the original use of the word was lost. Instead of describing an instant shot from a gun it was now associated with cameras.

One of Dr. Hodel's pastimes, a hobby he maintained from college, was driving around the city taking pictures. His long fingers gripped the wheel as he searched the street. Canvasing the area with his Flash Six-20 model Brownie, this camera was expensive in 1946, costing the doctor a whopping six dollars a pop. Considered high-end, this heavier, all-metal version was modeled in a tapered box with a curved film plane at the rear, with very little ornamentation, it was solid and tough and built like a tank and the most unlikely of weapons.

If Dr. Hodel had to, the best description would link it to fishing. Going from bus stop to bus stop, he watched waitresses get off from work and women hurrying on the street. Sitting at the Biltmore, Dr. Hodel's eyes kept darting to the door, but Elizabeth Short never walked in. So when the houselights came on announcing the 2:00 am curfew, Dr. Hodel went home and after working at his home office, began his canvasing again.

"Good morning."

A young Chinese girl looked around.

"Hello," he said louder, leaning across the passenger seat. The girl glanced at him and her uniform inched up her knees.

Dr. Hodel opened his door and got out of his car. Holding his Kodak, he approached the girl on the bench.

"Hi there!" snap snap snap. "I'm doing a story on immigrants in the city." snap snap

"Where were you born?" snap

"Where do you go to school? snap

"Your skin is as smooth as an oyster," snap snap, wind.

Feeling embarrassed, the Chinese girl turned away.

"Wait a minute. Don't be shy. USC paid me to take pictures."

Dr. Hodel didn't know where these lies came from, they just poured from his mouth like water.

The girl tried to ignore Hodel and turned the other way.

Dr. Hodel came closer taking more pictures of the girl's face and then lowered the camera down to her legs.

"You're such a beautiful creature." Snap.

The girl smiled. Most young girls do. Oh, there were a few wise crackers, a few worn tires who already knew the score but most girls in Los Angeles, anywhere between pigtails and a Playtex griddle, viewed a man driving an expensive car as "potential" and most of them popped up like toasters.

Just then, a fat Chinese man burst from store. He was Chinese too and started speaking to the girl. The girl looked scared and started to shake her head.

"Leave lone! gotdamnasama beech!" the Chinese man screamed, slamming one of his fists on Hodel's car.

Back in his car, he watched the girl's face fade in his rear view mirror. Heading toward work, he clicked his radio on and there was Strauss playing 'Blue Danube' instantly brightening his mood.

Driving four more blocks, he saw another girl on a bench.

Pulling up to the curb, Dr. Hodel put the car in park. "Hello!" he said talking over the motor. "I apologize for being so forward but I just had to stop to say, you're the most beautiful thing that I've ever seen."

The first thing Elizabeth noticed was his car. After the sugar sanctions and austerity measures during the war were finally over, Ford designed an upscale vehicle to tout the country's new wealth. The Mark II Lincoln Continental was a car to behold. A sign of triumph, a sign of power or fame it was a four-wheeled machine that screamed 'I have money.'

Smiling in order to hide a row of bad teeth, Elizabeth re-crossed her legs, hiking her dress up a notch. This car could be her ticket. Whoever driving it was rich. Extending her legs she widened her grin but quit smiling when she saw it was Dr. Hodel. Meeting him at his clinic, Elizabeth dated him once and ditched him to avoid having sex. If her hungry level wasn't so high she'd have never looked his way. But her stomach muscles started to scream, growling so loud she thought he could hear. Maybe she could get this loser to spring for an early dinner. He was ok looking, even at twenty years older. The kind of geezer who felt getting a girl her age was fine, maybe even his right. At least he wasn't a G.I. G.I.'s were cheap. They hated buying anything more than a nickel beer, thinking they could bankroll a roll in hay for one Schlitz. Men had been riding up on Elizabeth a long time. Tall for her age, it had been happening since she was 11. There was always a supply of lying, cheating scumbags anxious to give a girl a "lift." There were millions of them on every street corner in L.A. Some of them were filthy pigs, screaming from the street as if she were a bitch in heat. She'd been in Los Angeles less than a year and had already seen this routine a million times. She could handle these fiends. She'd knew how to finesse a brute.

She'd make sure she was good and fed and then give him the slip which served them right trying to get it so easy. So even though she knew she was taking a chance, her plan was to just get fed. All she wanted was to sit in a nice restaurant and rest. She took a long appreciative look at his car again. Obviously he had plenty of money. Rich men didn't roll up on you everyday. A rich man could open a door for a lonely girl like her. Maybe an opportunity hid under those white hands on the steering wheel. It could happen. She'd seen it happen to some of her friends. Well maybe not seen it but she certainly heard about it happening. Ann Toth, who came from nothing, was living in a mansion with the man who ran the Hollywood Palladium. Elizabeth snuck a sideways look at Dr. Hodel again. A man like him could mean one minute you're sitting on a bench starving to death and the next minute you're eating steak. Elizabeth looked down the street. A girl with a tight skirt was walked her way. Why should she give this bimbo a chance? This was the reason why she picked this bus bench. The Wilshire line was extremely busy. It was also a street caring the cars of wealthiest men. If she sat long enough, she could easily score lunch or dinner. Elizabeth leaned forward. She watched Dr. Hodel face. He wore the expression of a Catholic priest, kind-hearted and pure. Elizabeth pointed her long legs at his car door. Maybe he was her savior.

Elizabeth gave him her best Marlene Dietrich stare. While butterflies thumped her stomach, she teased, "Take a picture it lasts longer."

As soon as the words left her lips Elizabeth felt strange. "Stop worrying," she told herself. "You handled him before." Forcing herself to appear stronger than she really felt inside flooded her cheekbones with heat.

"You're blushing," Dr. Hodel said. Grabbing his camera, he snapped a shot. "You have the most radiant skin I've ever seen," he said. "My goodness it's almost translucent."

Leaning forward a bit, Elizabeth instinctively struck a pose.

Dr. Hodel wilted inside. He hated when it was too easy. He lived for the chase. Capturing unsuspecting prey was the greatest rush. That's why he didn't like brothels. Brothels were a brain-numbing bores. In a brothel, you already knew everyone line by heart. Every woman inside said whatever he wanted to hear. What kind of conquest was that? Nothing surpassed capturing a girl on the street. The street provided exciting new conquests each day. The ultimate rush for Hodel was the struggle of wills. He thrilled for the battle of two diametrically opposing goals. Only then, could he finally feel vibrant. Only in conquest could he feel that satisfying gush inside his blood. Using his brain to figure out a way in made his soar. And even though his game often drew blood, he never had so much fun.

Dr. Hodel eyed her smile. He watched her fingers claw the bench. *Careful, boy*, he warned himself. *Don't scare her off. Don't blow it by being too aggressive!*

He waited. He made himself take his time. Breathing deeply, he forced himself to go slow as his fingernails clawed the camera's box.

That's right. Easy does it, boy.

Like an actor reading a script, he enunciated every line. Acting as if she were the female lead, or a beautiful cat caught in a tree, he modulated his speech to woo her in.

"That's a lovely dress," he said. "It compliments your hair."

To calm himself down, he mentally measured her dimensions. Thighs: 19.5. Weigh: 115. Neck 10.5 or 11. While measuring each cheekbone and calculating the length of her femur, he channeled Man Ray and Marcel Duchamp. They told him everything was an illusion. Nothing in life was real. This surrealism philosophy made Dr. Hodel smile. How could he be sure he was sitting in his car? How did he know if this girl was really sitting on that bench? That's why during the incest trial he told the jury he couldn't remember. Maybe he touched his daughter, he couldn't be entirely sure. Like the opium dens of his youth, all the details seemed foggy and blurry. Maybe he performed fellatio. It was all still a blur, like a mirror going foggy during a shower. There was one thing he did know for sure. His no-good-big-mouth-daughter should have kept her mouth shut. Luckily his attorney put her inside a women's shelter. Locked for ten months, by the time the trial started, his daughter was a year older and no longer a kid. When she finally took the stand after she was so shell-shocked she could barely talk. Dressed in a crimson sweater and leggy pencil skirt, his attorney took the extra step to platinum blond her hair making her look like bombshell instead of a kid claiming incest. Hodel smiled to himself. Jerry Geisler was the best. This was the same attorney who helped Errol Flynn escape a rape charge. Flynn was in the middle of a swashbuckling career. *The Adventures of Robin Hood* made him a star and he was set to act in the *Adventures of Don Juan*. His rape trial shocked nation. The city wanted blood. "Hang Him!" the *L.A. Times* headlines screamed. But Geisler was smart. He packed the jury with loyal Flynn fans. Obtaining an acquittal, "In like Flynn" became a popular phrase for anyone who escaped trouble. Even after befriending another underage girl during the trial, even after Geisler begged him to stay saying "Don't sleep with her until the case is over," he ordered. Flynn took the girl home during the trial and after a wild night of cocaine and whiskey, brutally raped her. Knowing he'd never survive the scandal, Flynn slipped across the border, marrying the girl to prevent her from ever pressing charges.

Hodel did feel a tad nervous when his daughter said the sex started at ten. He remembered one of the jurors looked at him and raised a brow. During that part of the trial detachment became a stretch. He felt naked. Every follicle surged. He suffered through the event by channeling Marcel Duchamp. Duchamp was the most detached man he ever met. Duchamp didn't display one iota of emotion. Even if a firing squad exploded in Duchamp's chest he could remain in a perfect surrealistic calm, like the Pacific Ocean at dawn. Hodel strived to be a surrealist. Surrealists rejected feelings. Feelings got in the way of doing what you wanted. Feelings enabled him to hear begs and screams. Surrealism allowed him to create without the pain of being humane.

When Elizabeth crossed her legs, Hodel squeezed his butt cheeks, a gesture he could do without being seen. Each gesture reflected the opposite of what he felt inside. In the vein of feigning calm and hiding a bestial masculinity, Hodel measured his speech, he ignored the fly that buzzed near his ear. Appearing as calm as melting ice, he hid the jackhammer inside. Turning his voice into the sweet timbre of Concerto No. 5. he disguised a basement of breaking plates. Batting his doe-like eyes, he fiddled with the gold band on his hand, like a married man stepping out for the very first time.

Dr. Hodel watched Elizabeth Short open the door. Gliding her thighs across the vinyl seat, he stared ahead as she climbed inside. Hearing the click of the car lock made him almost explode and it took everything he had to remain composed.

During a quick turn, Elizabeth slid near his chest. For a split second, she felt a stabbing pang of regret. Something felt wrong. Something was off. She immediately remembered the weird feeling she felt before. Even though he spoke low, like a priest mumbling a prayer, his huge engine squawked like an electrical saw, dissecting the base of a tree.

Heading west, passing a hotdog stand, he asked if she wanted a Coke?

Elizabeth shook her head no.

Driving faster than anyone should around curves, he suddenly took it slow and headed into the Hollywood hills where he turned off a dangerous road.

"Have you ever been to Rustic Canyon?" he asked.

"No," she said, "I haven't seen the pier either," Elizabeth suggested, wishing for the openness of the beach instead of a dark looming canyon.

Dr. Hodel didn't hear her. He was totally lost in thought. After another treacherous bend, he stopped the car and pulled over.

"I love gates." Hodel said, parking in front of wrought-iron rusty gate guarding what seemed like a fortress.

Dr. Hodel stepped out of the car, walked over to the gate. Gliding his hands on the gate's railing as if holding the tail of a cat, he said, "This was designed by architect Paul Williams." Unhooking the latch, he lifted it up and pushed the gate open. "Welcome to Murphy's Ranch," he said.

Elizabeth paused a second before opening the car's door.

Pushing the gate open further, he went on. "This is where a community of Nazis lived to wait out the war."

Opening the gate all the way he took a few steps down the staircase. "Don't you want to see it?" he beckoned.

Getting out the car slowly, she walked to the beginning of an enclave known as Murphy Ranch. Behind the rusted wrought-iron entrance gates was an entire flagstone wall and staircase dropping down 500 steps. Traces of a small community that occupied the space remained. There was a dam, a gigantic debris-filled swimming pool, a circular concrete tank used to store water, a greenhouse, and a dam catching the natural spring water from a creek.

Peering down, Elizabeth couldn't see any of these things except a staircase dropping into blackness.

"Do you want to see it!" he beckoned, taking a few steps down.

Elizabeth tried her best to return Dr. Hodel's smile. The staircase looked dangerous and the place was totally remote. She didn't want to go down there with him. "I don't know," Elizabeth smiled and rubbed her stomach instead. "I guess I'm just really hungry."

"Oh," Dr. Hodel said, a little disappointed. He rushed to her side of the door and held it open and waited for her to slid in.

When they finally got out of the hills, Elizabeth exhaled slowly. She hadn't realized she'd been holding her breath. It felt good to let a bit of air enter her lungs and see the city lights again.

Driving aimlessly, Dr. Hodel drove down La Brea Blvd. heading south. Turning left on Rodeo Road he was now on a wide street called Santa Barbara Blvd. Making a left on Degnan, he noticed an empty lot filled with weeds where construction was continuing in an area called Leimert Park. Dr. Hodel drove by this street twice. Backtracking he took Jefferson and headed east. Chatting incessantly, useless words sputtered out of his mouth.

blah,blah,blah, blah,blah,blah, blah,blah,blah,blah.

. Suddenly they were in front of The Shrine Auditorium downtown.

Peering at the majestic building, a mist fell across Hodel's eyes. "I used to play in this Shrine auditorium as a child." While at the stoplight, he closed his eyes, humming a piano concerto and was totally lost in time. "I was only eight," he said in a voice younger than before. "Naturally, I was enormously flattered to be on stage." He clicked the radio on, and Rachmaninoff playing *Liszt's 2nd Hungarian Rhapsody* flooded the car.   Hodel lifted one hand fingering an imaginary piano. Music was the only thing that soothed him. Music immediately put him at ease. He was so calm, he didn't see the light change to green. The car behind him started an angry concerto of its own. Coming out of his haze, Hodel looked up and picked up speed. When the car-honk guy jumped in front, Hodel rushed by his side, causing the car-honk guy to veer off of the road.

Fearful of crashing, Elizabeth tried to calm him down. "You still play?" she prodded, smiling while he raced.

Dr. Hodel snapped his fingers near Elizabeth's ear, "I stopped just like that. Never touched the piano again." He felt a familiar anger rising up in his throat and it was difficult to force it back down.

Gripping the steering wheel, the boy-voice disappeared. "It was difficult for mother to understand my indifference. But frankly, I lived my entire life as if treading on eggshells. Mother tried to turn my piano playing into her personal success by pawning me off on her friends. I had to play for luncheons. I had to give private concerts on their lawns or in drawing rooms as stuffy as tombs. I quit all of it once mother was out of the picture."

That was the phrase that made her glance at him again. He wasn't looking at her or squeezing the steering wheel tight anymore. He looked happy. He looked pleased with himself. Like it thrilled him to know his mother was gone. People shouldn't talk like that about their mothers. And what did 'out of the picture' mean exactly? Did he do something to her? Was he the one who made sure she was gone? Breathing deeply Elizabeth tried to calm herself down. If she had a nickel for every married man who hated his past, she'd already be a millionaire.

It was January. Elizabeth felt a cool breeze underneath her skirt. Watching the palm trees doing back bends against the wind, she began to feel more and more queasy. Maybe she was overreacting. Maybe she was paranoid like her roommates claimed. Sometimes she slept in theaters when she didn't have a cent. She'd sit through the same scary movie again and again until an usher came, shook her shoulder and made her leave. Come on, Elizabeth told herself, get a grip! Not everyone is a psycho. Not everyone is a vampire who wants to bite your throat.

To avoid thinking the worst, Elizabeth focused on his car. She stared at the wood grain dashboard. She looked at the metal pole of his gearshift. She glimpsed her own face in the side-view mirrors. His car was immaculate. The seat was genuine leather. Like him, the outside was clean and showpiece neat. And the truth was, she was getting nowhere alone on that bench except priming herself for a case of bronchitis. Taking a deep breath and exhaling slow, Elizabeth's stomach growled again and she placed her hand over her abdomen. Glancing at her surroundings she didn't recognize these streets. Looking at the doctor she asked if they were getting close.

"Doctor," Elizabeth asked. "Is the Biltmore far from here?"

"Please, no formalities," Dr. Hodel placed his arm around her seat. "Call me George," he said giving her shoulders a squeeze and staring intently in her face.

Smiling quickly, Elizabeth turned to look out her window. Some people still had Christmas decorations over their lawns. A cherub faced Santa dressed in red grinned at her face, his black belt sectioned his body in two.

"I love winter," the doctor said wistfully breathing in the Eucalyptus trees. "We're taking the scenic route through West Adams. I love these old mansions. They remind me of the homes in Pasadena where I grew up. My bedroom faced east. The Biltmore faces eastward too." Dr. Hodel smiled at Elizabeth's anxious face. "Don't worry, darling, we're close. See, here's Figueroa."

A majestic hotel appeared in front of Dr. Hodel's car.

"The Biltmore serves the best steaks in the world," he said.

And just like that it was done. One minute she was at a bus stop freezing to death and the next minute she was in car heading toward a juicy steak. And even though she could see the sky and the trees whizzing by, a tingling feeling kept creeping up her neck. She watched stop signs go by like chance after chance and although she sat as erect as a Christmas tree in front of a window, Elizabeth felt like she was sinking in sand. Suddenly she began chattering like mad. As if talking would make It fine. A world-wind of words started tumbling across her tongue. And then it hit, like a ton of bricks or Mac truck slamming into a concrete wall. The smell of his cologne felt violently wrong. The male scent reminded her of everything her mother ever said. The warning. The mantra. A cautionary tale all girls learn by heart. DON'T EVER GET INTO A STRANGE MAN'S CAR. But now it's too late. She ripped a hangnail off her thumb. Because face it, it's her fucking fault she was here. She knew as soon as she saw him. She knew when the car pulled up. She knew as soon as woke up that morning and still she was unable to stop it.

The Death of the Truth About Death

Made one with Death

Filled full of the Night

                      -Algernon Swinburne

We bow to the Truth,

but it won't scrape us by.

Not that Death lurks behind all smiles,

Dirges fattening Basses with baseless,

smiling Masques of Death,

Red and unread.

So I burn. I stare from afar,

from a feasible summit.

Peering down

at the top of Death's headlight,

ringed in florid falsifying

flame-suckled hoodies

and

Death's dread-me knots.

The Master said:

Komm, süßer Tod,

  komm sel'ge Ruh

But Bach was wrong:

"Sweet' Death" is not

"blessed rest".

It may be sweet

to your touch –

but only if life is not.

So it is Life

        just Life - stems your sad

            and lonely burning.

I must have Death as it is. Horrible,

hot Handiwork of Heavenly

happenstance. Macabre Finality

at the End of the Lifeline.

The Sweetness of Nothing.

Till then it hurts.

Martin Perlich

Yeast

    Marques died in front of me that day for no reason at all. Just a bunch of black boys running around with guns, shooting other black boys in the name of a gang. I never understood the comradery of gangs. I mean, creating a family not necessarily by blood and protecting it by rules of engagement and politics that supposedly superseded societal norms, and expectations all in the name of honor. But I guess it's no different than the white founding fathers of the United States, people coming together for a perceived common good and willing to fight to the death for their ideologies. But gangs? Gangs played by their own rules and that day they decided they wanted Marques two weeks before our high school graduation.

    Marques was chocolate, six foot three, and every bit of the basketball player his height would suggest. On the court, he wore his huge afro in a puffed pony tail on top of his head to show off his "good hair", because he knew every girl in the school would be watching and every boy, like Dominique, would be jealous. The funny thing is we looked alike, despite the fact I was a girl and he towered over me in height. We were both "pretty" and I was athletic like him. We used to joke about our parents being swingers and not letting us know that we were really brother and sister. The day of Edmond's kickback we wore our hair down, frizzy and all with our matching "Retro-ed "Air Jordan Concord 11's on. We ended up leaving early though because we both agreed there were too many drugs being passed around. Marques and I decided long ago that we weren't going out like that. Besides, our new Jordan's were on foot patrol because neither one of us had a car and it was getting too dark to see.

    When we realized Dominique and three other boys were following us, things got real. We knew that they were from a gang, so we switched up and ran down the back road, thinking we could outrun them to the grocery store. Marques whispered "Hurry up and run in front of me". I'm sure since I was a girl he was trying to protect me. I got to the brick wall first and he instinctually grabbed me like a boy and shoved me up until I could swing my body over the top of the wall. "Wait for me, I'll be right back". I heard that black superhero voice before but now was not the time. I dropped down and landed hard watching for him to follow. Finally, Marques swung one leg over and then the other as if in a sitting position at the top of the wall. He looked down, met my eyes, winked and said "I think I lost them", then shots raged out of nowhere, BOOM, BOOM- BOOM, BOOM.

Marques' expression changed frozen in time with a look of disbelief as the bullets tore through his neck and back. His shoulders curved forward and his stomach sank in. I watched my best friend fall backwards with his knees locked tightly around the top of the wall. Dominique and his friends laughed as the back of Marques' head smashed into the other side of the wall. I heard someone say "Damn that shit smashed like a pumpkin". On my side all I could see was Marques' Jordan's digging into the bricks. The laughs stopped as if they realized what they had done. Another voice said "We got that nigga good". "Oh my God, Oh my God, Let's go! Let's go!". Through the wall, I could hear Marques struggling to breathe.

I frantically searched for a way back over what seemed like a twenty- foot wall. I found a crate to support my weight but it still wasn't enough to get my five foot two frame to the top of the wall. I reached for the only thing I could, Marques' legs as his feet continued to dig into the bricks like he knew I needed them to get to the top. I slipped my fingers around his chiseled calf and pulled myself to the wall's top and fell over to find Marques hanging upside down, arms spread out like black Jesus on an inverted cross. I tried to pull him down but his knees remained locked firmly in place. All I could do was hold his head up as warm, red, rain sprayed from the side of his neck baptizing me, marking me for life. There were no sirens, no help came, just me witnessing the final seconds of a life once lived now gone.

Over the years, I thought about Marques every day. Two of the boys were caught and went to prison while the other two, ironically were murdered in another act of violence. I thought about them though. I thought about some of the other boys in my school going to jail for selling drugs, trying to survive day to day. Some, few of them, left the dry little town we grew up in on the outskirts of Los Angeles county and went to college outside of California, for something better.

Me? I stayed out of shock, grief, or just the serious desire to get to know myself better in familiar surroundings. I think I lost hope in everything. I grew tired of watching the black boys and men in my life disappear. It seemed like a process of elimination switch had been continuously flicked on, whether through self- infliction, police brutality, or natural selection in the environment, somehow labeling being a black man with Failure to Thrive Syndrome. So I stayed away from my beautiful black men, all men as a matter of fact. I stayed as far away as I could until one day a little nappy headed, ashy, seven- year old boy appeared in my life. He needed me and I didn't know it then, but I definitely needed him. This, all of this, is his story.

Kimberly Evans

I am clay

May 17th, 2012

I am clay —

Liquid and weak.

I have neither tongue

Nor mouth, to speak.

Everyone likes

To make some figure

To make a shape

From me.

I am clay —

Liquid and weak.

I always go

Through palms.

I leak…

I leak…

Azam Obidov

Perhaps, for Bulabeck Deng, a Dreamsong

Bulabeck Deng in his dream

knows that there's a hostile

pack of hyena in the

rear of the yard,

just near the alley.

And Bulabeck Deng turns over

and over in his restless bed.

ii

Bulabeck Deng asleep on his quivering

back, peeping out from

under his quilt and

hearing them approach

as he counts

one hyena

two hyena

three

then a fourth one appears:

Primal attack forcefully

grouping itself

angry green-eyed stares

snarling,first;

then watching

their prey

shaking and weakening

well into the night.

iii

hyena one now at the back

door sniffing about, vaguely knowing

that this unmoving house

must be attacked.

hyena two, upstairs now, wondering

if perhaps a new level of

attack is in order: its snout smile, its confidence

unchallenged.

hyenas three and four have already

attacked a small fearful domestic

cat.

iv

The scene: the freshly

killed cat and Bulabeck Deng

and the four hyena and

that rancid smell

that follows death

as Bulabeck Deng suddenly re-calls his

mother:[at times one

calls out, quite viscerally ,

for one's mother, whether dead

or alive, doesn't one?]

v

Bulabeck Deng perspires:

wonders about his next

dream and what it

might reveal.

his is new fear

that hungry hyena bring

is unlike all other spheres,

eh?

vi

Bulabeck Deng thinks

perhaps only senses

a certain vague

moistness on his ankle.

One of the invading predators,

perhaps? Or worse: the unexampled,

blind fear that his friend Peter Kwal

had warned him about. Simple enough,

that.

vii

Bulabeck Deng has this

longing for a weapon

sufficient for the killing of one hyena:

the brutal killing of one hyena, just one, and hopefully

the others would flee. Do not freeze.

Waiting, while being preyed upon, is madness.

Do not freeze. One's senses must always be alert.

Do not freeze.

Phillip B Middleton

God is sleeping

The old serpent is sitting on my shoulder,
I cannot open my eyes,
I cannot open my lips
to thank God.
In addition to this it's raining.
I am growing stout – what is more.
God is sleeping in my heavy heart.
***

The soul fills with liberty
Keen light looks like your sad hope
You never dreamt of

Azam Obidov

Cartography in California

Cartography in California

History shows us the life of nations and finds nothing to narrate but wars and tumults; the peaceful years appear only as brief pauses and interludes.
- Schopenhauer.

<u>I The establishment of measurements:</u>
<u>Madrid to Los Angeles</u>

In the beginning,
they came from Spain.
Some from Madrid.
Some from Barcelona.
An old Spanish monk
walked up the coastline
cutting out the El Camino Real.

Serra planted seeds
for
       San Diego,
       San Juan Capistrano
       La Ciudad de Los Angeles.
He planted small viruses
that multiplied and killed their host cells.
List victims of dna infections.
List endangered family trees:
       Yokuts,
       Yahi,
       Wintu,
       Wintun
       Monache,
       Chumash.

On sanctified grounds,

rose the Spanish Empire.
Decades later,
it became Mexico.
Decades later,
it became the United States.
Decades later, it will become the land of Bladerunners,
a garden covered in concrete, glass, and people.
The trees will never grow back.

Houses grow here,
but the houses are not designed to last.
They are designed to collapse over time
as they poison their inhabitants with radon.

II
A measurement of dreaming:
San Salvador to Los Angeles

"Your application for residency has been declined.
You are not a political refugee.
Your government is recognized as an ally."

Return home.
Bullets hit random people
walking from one village to another.
After they raped and killed the Maryknoll sisters,
the assassination game was hurried.
Bishops were expendable.

A woman
      clutches her child
      decides to walk to El Norte.
The father has disappeared.
He is probably under an unmarked field
covered by grass and leaves by his brother's body.

Cross the rainforests of Central America.
Walk across
      Chiapas territory.
      Old Mayan lands.
      Old Aztec capitals.
Walk across fences.
Walk across to the land of angels.

In a desert
sell cut mangos
            on a cart with a bell.
Hope your child
does not follow
the 18th Street-way,
another way to enforce gangster rules.

Rent a room
overlooking MacArthur Park.
Watch a man selling forgetfulness
in a plastic bag.

Realize
he too came from the same village.
He escaped,
but he haunts a park
with an artificial lake.
How many bodies are underneath there?

Soccer games go on
even if the grass is already dead.

The sound of children echoes into the twilight
A gunfight erupts across the street
A child dies; it is the same as before.

III
A measurement of exile:
Hong Kong to Los Angeles

The end of the British Empire:
The wealthiest colony
will go back to China.
So ends a fruitful life
after the Opium Wars.

The old ways of requiring leaders
to pass a test
      on writing poetry,
        on quoting the sages
has long been over.
Read instead the memoirs of Mao.
Where is your copy of the Red Book?

A Hong Kong woman
with a British accent,
tells a Sansei man,
"Oxford was pleasant."
"Will you ever return to Hong Kong?"
"No. My family is here now in Alhambra, dear."

Alhambra, California.
Pipe dream of a Chinese realtor.
Now a city full of
      Chinese restaurants.
      Chinese herbal shops.
      Chinese markets.

He asks her,
"Do you wish you could be in England?"
"Yes, but they are restricting immigration."
He asks her
"Do you want to see Los Angeles?"

"What do you have here?"

"Everything and nothing . . .
The city changes constantly.
Years ago, Koreatown was a dream too.
We can find any type of food now.
Have your tried Korean tofu?"

IV
A measurement of collapse:
Budapest to Los Angeles

A Hungarian man tells a Sansei man
about a peculiar way of eating slices of bread--
bacon grease and sugar.
"No butter?"
"Bacon grease is wonderful.
You should try it.
In Budapest, the food is not expensive.
But the rent is very high for a Westerner."

Hungarians must love strongly spiced foods.
We are eating chicken infused heavily
with garlic and onions.
A dark red wine from Hungary is shared.
It tastes much better with the food.
Hungarian blood wine.

In the background,
a group of Turks are dancing
to a new song from Istanbul.
My Budapest comrade tells me,
"You can not have a party without the Turks.
Watch their hands roll with the songs.
The feet rarely move.
They can dance forever."

Next to us,
a Polish man is speaking Russian
to a Muscovite.
He turns around and translates,
"Crime in Moscow is pretty bad.
Warsaw was not pleasant either."
They return to Russian words.
They are drinking Coronas with limes.

The Budapest man says,
"If I ever go back, come visit.
You can ride the train
To Czechland or Germany."
I look around and think--
Bacon grease and sugar?

"How is the poetry scene there?"

"You must go to Prague, my friend.
You must go to Kafka's city."

V
A measurement of a mother's devotion:
Tehran to Los Angeles

We are sitting at a table,
with saffron rice and pickled eggplants.
Nilofaur, her daughter,
was named after a flower in Iran; she
is telling her mom about her day at school.
This 10 year old encapsulates an entire map
of a changing world.

To save my flower
I had to fly
from Tehran to New Delhi.
There was a problem with Nilofaur's aorta.
I had to gather up funds, acquire a visa.

The Indian doctors
Couldn't treat her.
A nurse told me
it could be handled in America.
I had a friend from the same village
now in America.
I called.

My daughter,
3 years old,
didn't understand travel.
After I flew back to Tehran,
I made arrangements.

Then came the time
to walk to Istanbul.
Crossed the lands of the Kurds
into the lands of the Turks.
I wore blue.

Not just any blue, turquoise blue.
The Turkish say, it keeps evil away.
(So began the history of a turquoise pendant.)

At last,
At the American Embassy.
I stated that she had a medical problem.
Now the waiting.
A month of care
grew a new visa.

Flew to Berlin.
Train to Paris.
Flew to Heathrow Airport.
Flew to New York.

I presented my visa to customs.
Called up my friend.
She traced out a way to get to Los Angeles.
On the way,
I tired to learn some decent English.
I arrived in Downtown LA.
Forgotten friends greeted each other.
I rested in a borrowed room,
while looking through magazines
written in a language to be read
left to right.
Nilofaur was confused.
My friend called the hospital in Loma Linda.
She drove us
into the heart of Inland Empire.

My daughter underwent open heart surgery.
I waited in waiting room.

> *She came out of surgery.*
> *She had a large scar*

> *which marked a split ribcage.*

Will my Nilofaur grow up into the blooming flower?

7 years later,
         a Sansei man is eating
saffron rice with the map-makers.

"Do you miss Iran?"
"Yes, but I must stay here."
"Don't you like not having to wear the veil?"

"You can wear the veil and still be pretty.
But everyone is here.
My husband and Faramarz.
Nilofaur is growing here.

We can't go back."

David Maruyama

THE SERPENT IN THE BARN RAFTERS

Why did the serpent try again to ascend to heaven, fail
and settle then on caged light, its stomach filled with mortality?

It was on a Sunday morning when looking up I spied
Lucifer twined around the glowing bulb; his own convenient sun.

The warmth of the caged bulb provided him a bright heaven.
Though he could not constrict this prey he could enjoy its blessing.

His flickering tongue told him tales of feathered fluttering tension.
Had he wings he'd have flown from nest to nest in gluttonous joy.

When down from temptation's height he fell to earth again, there
disturbed by footsteps, he raised his head to challenge my intrusion.

The fallen beast was burdened with prey and so could not slither by.
There in the hay its black mottled skin rippled like light on a bright pond.

The garden it found itself in this day mirrored its ancient demise,
 but when he spoke to Eve this time she heard nothing.

Adam arrived with tools used to change the course of rivers and history.
His angry spade opened the snake's body like it was a clump of moist clay

and revealed, its last meal—a swallow, a fledgling, consumed whole
like a shooting star in a dark sky suddenly overwhelmed by clouds.

Is it in the deaths of snakes we see sin removed from the world
and in their dispatch, spade in hand, we stand naked again before God?

What is the taste of that fruit we hope to pluck from our effort?
Is it the pomegranate's sweetness, or the apple's forbidden literacy?

It doesn't matter. That slender creature is death's captive now,
and soon another, seeking heaven's bounty, will ascend to these rafters.

George Edward Buggs

THADDEUS GOTDOE pt2

A tale of a vampire

Chapter Two
Together again

Thaddeus stared at his mirror for a long time. He thought he'd noticed his reflection didn't seem as sharp as it once did. It never failed, when he was in the mirror he had to force himself from it. Little did he know, the more he embraced being a vampire, his reflection in the mirror would fade away until it was no longer visible.

It was a bitter/sweet moment for him, because he truly liked his single man status, but his love and need for Allison far outweighed his single life. Even though he had quite a few women, he fancied himself an eligible bachelor and loved his freedom.

Finally, he compelled himself to leave the mirror and continue to get dressed to meet with his heart, for lunch. Even though he reluctantly was going to meet with her, he knew full well once this meeting was completed, Allison more than likely would be moving in with him. She made all the right moves, although Thaddeus countered each one of them with ease. Even so, that did nothing for the lust he still had for her.

After seeing him that morning at the golf course with his golfing buddies, Allison began calling Thaddeus. She started right out trying to seduce him over the phone, to no avail. When that didn't work she actually came to his home, but Thaddeus knew to play hard. He didn't even respond to the door bell ringing, knowing full well it was Allison.

She tried to get into his head through telepathy, but he blocked her mental tactics, countering her telepathy with seductive thoughts and phrases of his own. With vampires, it was all about the lust they held for their mate. Even if the mates were not in the same space, they could feel each other's presence; but this had to be developed over time and if done properly they could communicate even being oceans apart.

Thaddeus didn't know he could feel Allison, but knew she could somehow feel him, but by her being a young vampire also, she hadn't mastered it. Still, she was far from the manipulator she would become in the short future. She was in the early stages of being a vampire and all of her abilities were not fully developed, but of those that had, seduction was prevalent.

Over the years that she had been away from Thaddeus she matured into a woman of sheer beauty and filled with a vampire's desires. For her, being married to Daniel was an ongoing battle because in doing so, she denied her true self all that time. It was difficult for her, even though she visited her grandfather's ranch three or four times a week to feed and relieve her tensions.

There, she would nourish her body on his many cattle to satisfy her thirst for blood. When visiting her grandfather, they often spoke of her marriage and how unhappy she was. The only benefit for her was after her feedings Daniel would be the recipient of some of the wildest sex he ever had and she could let some of her aggression out under the guise of sex.

That day when she saw Thaddeus for the first time at the golf course, her inner self was immediately awakened and she could not stand being in the presence of her husband after that. It took Thaddeus denying her, for her to realize she needed a strong man. A man qualified in all regards and able to deal with the woman she had become. She knew she wanted Thaddeus.

Allison knew she actually needed him, but she would not cave in easily. Only after all of her vixen ways failed, did one day she call Thaddeus and cry her heart out to him in a last ditch attempt to seduce him. It wasn't easy for her to do, because in doing so she made herself vulnerable to him.

Vampires have feelings, but their thoughts of carnage mostly suppress them. If a vampire allows their feelings to surface, even for a moment, it opens a door to control them and Thaddeus seized the opportunity he was waiting for to dominate her. He quietly listened to her plea for his attention.

"Thaddeus, I have left my husband and am filing for a divorce. I don't need his money or status; I need you. As long as I never saw you, I thought I could be over you. Now that I have, you're all I can think about. Please Thaddeus . . . don't make me beg you . . . don't make this more difficult for me than it already is."

He gloated a moment, realizing she was at the thresh hole of surrendering, before he said to her, "Hold on Allison, my skilled actress. I am not one for a lot of dramatics and am obviously not the weak vampire you thought I was, so you can save the tears for someone else. I have enjoyed my life and have been able to experience it without you. I do however . . . my beautiful black, rose; think I am better with you, than without you."

At that moment Allison perked up and listened with great anticipation as he finished his statement. She felt he was on the verge of inviting her in. One thing that remained constant with all vampires, they must be invited in for them to be able to get you under their spells.

"So, if you can get your blooming beauty over here in the next few minutes, I may be just what the doctor ordered for you, you understand . . . hello? Allison, are you there?"

Allison was in full anticipation of this response and before he could complete the sentence, she had hung up the phone and raced to her car. Quickly, she started it and sped backwards out of the driveway. As she did she floored it and careened around the corner heading to the freeway, driving almost like a maniac.

After the ten mile drive, she exited the freeway and screeched to a halt at the stop sign. She peeled off from the stop and raced through South San Francisco, rounding the last corner before she could see his house. She was so excited to be able to see Thaddeus Gotdoe again, she could not contain herself. As she screeched to a halt, before the car was fully stopped, she leaped out.

Quickly, she hurried up the walkway and as she raised her hand to ring the doorbell, Thaddeus opened the door. For a moment, they stared at one another, before he invited her in. She walked in slowly and Thaddeus, now a seasoned vampire looked at his soul mate and began seducing her with his glare. She started stripping and as she did her K9s elongated, as did his.

The K9s extending signaled a challenge, but by no means would he allow her to succeed in any type of positioning. His eyes became pitch black and as they did he also became aroused to the point, he dropped his pants and his meat poked straight ahead. He approached her and when they met, their fangs glistened with saliva and each of their tongues began to slowly come out of their mouths.

As per the ritual, they started moving in a small circle, each jockeying to gain control of their stare. After they had gone a full circle, they began licking each other's tongue continuing to circle as they did. They turned slowly as their long tongues wrapped around the others in this ritualistic type dance.

After a few moments of this, he was able to lock eyes with her as they continued to slowly go in a circle, licking tongues, until she could stand it no more. Only full vampires knew of this ritual and it only excited natural mates. A vampire with interest in another vampire could lure and seduce a permanent mate with this dance.

Allison's eyes darkened and her sultry features hardened as she grabbed him and they kissed. To show his strength, he had to outlast her in this show down until she fully submitted. Until she turned into a vampire and submitted to him, he was not in control of her. He watched her beauty turn hard and as he kissed her, he could feel her becoming his mate in entirety.

The entire time they were together in the streets of San Francisco, she had never fully turned, giving in to him as the dominant vampire. She had surrendered her clan of gypsy women to him, but not the control of her dark side. Now that Thaddeus had made her show her true self, after he had sex with her, as long as they lived she would never deny him.

Thaddeus studied and learned as much as he could about the life of a vampire and knew exactly how to establish full control. He knew the tongue move was like a standoff and the first one to break the lock was weakest and would always be submissive to the other. He also knew unless she showed her true self, he would never really control her. Allison knew this also and tried her best, but she wanted Thaddeus and could not hold out any longer.

"Take me my King," she requested.

"Take you I will, my precious black rose."

To seal this union, Thaddeus began the bite of love ritual vampires had. He positioned his woman in his arms and began to spin around. His speed quickened and Allison's legs left the ground and as Thaddeus spent her around, he sank his K9s into her neck. Then he prepared to have sex with her.

Being a more mature man without worry of performance, he tantalized her with his oral sex. He spoke to her as he played with her clitoris with his long tongue. Oral sex for Allison was always the best part for her, but this evening Thaddeus would take her to yet another level of pleasure. Since she was last with him, a lot of vampire had manifested in him; most notably his long snake like tongue and his pitch dark eyes when he was in the moment.

Thaddeus had learned to use his tongue to perfection. For Allison, he remembered she liked him to tease her clitoris before actually penetrating her. He placed his tongue on her clit and with the tip of it started massaging it. When she became moist from the stimulation, he stuck it inside of her, curled it up and licked the top of her tunnel until she could stand it no longer. Then he mounted her doggy style.

Before he did, he took his time and observed her glistening vagina, as he put the head of his penis inside her. She began moving, taking a little more, slowly. Each time she moved back towards him, he went in that much more until he was fully inside her. Since his tongue had become snakelike, he wiggled it inside her mouth, when they kissed. After a few minutes of this, Allison began to moan and as she did she began to convulse in climax. When she started climaxing she squirted juice out on her leg. Thaddeus felt her convulsing and this only promoted more from him as he pushed deeper inside her, until she almost fainted.

"Thaddeus, wait. You're too much for me to take at once. I can only handle what I can," she admitted as she lay on her back for a round of missionary style sex.

"Listen to me, my love. Promise me you will never leave me again."

For a vampire, it's not easy to get overly involved in an act of sex, or any emotional situation. They're cold and would prefer to stay distant, but when it was their mate bringing it out of them they couldn't control how they responded. She had already conceded to him, but he wanted her to do it in the heightened state of being her full dark self.

Both of them knew that the bond had already been sealed, but he wanted to be in a full vampire state and Allison would not willingly do it. The stronger vampire has to manipulate the weaker one, or lose the control. Almost everything they did with one another was some kind of challenge and it kept both of them thinking all of the time.

As Allison turned vampire, he saw his chance to forever have dominance over her. He needed her to recommit her loyalty to him while in a vampire state. As she grew closer to climax he continued speaking to her.

"You see I am no weakling and your shrewd ways will never work on me; so promise me also that you will always understand I am your King."

Thaddeus was ready for a mental battle, but to his surprise she turned vampire and agreed.

"I promise, Thaddeus. I promise I will never think of leaving you again and will always be at your side from here to eternity."

At that moment she leaned her neck to the side and Thaddeus bit her again. This time he didn't bite her to suck her blood; he was putting his mark on her. This was the second time they'd been apart, but it was a good time for the both of them to discover what they really wanted out of their life together. Neither of them knew this, but as they got along it became apparent that they were meant for each other.

The first time they were apart only lasted a few months, but Thaddeus was in his street life then and had so many women he didn't really care she was gone. He still has many women in his life, but now he is more serious about his being a vampire and his desires now more and more require the company of a true mate.

In his opinion, neither of his current women were worthy of being bitten and no matter what the case, the bottom line was he wanted Allison. Allison Vimpyre had what it takes to keep him happy and was the only woman for the vampire named, Thaddeus Gotdoe.

What Thaddeus wanted he usually always got and now that he had Allison again, his appetite for sex increased. His girlfriends numbered in the twenties and all would be the recipients of sex from a man with the prowess of an avid sex machine. He must have sex daily, because besides satisfying his libido, his women provided him sustenance.

He rarely ate food and when he did it was so people could see him eat, but his nourishment came from the blood he sucked from the women he dated. It had become a science for him now. He would have a different woman every night, as to not over feed on any one of them. Even with all of these women at his disposal, he could not remember the last time he was sexually satisfied.

As long as he didn't feed directly into their vein, or did not feed on them too often in a thirty day period, the women would simply be under his spell and enjoy some of the most pleasure filled sex they ever had. He, on the other hand was always in need of the kind of satisfaction only a true mate could give him; thusly his need for Allison grew, but he denied it.

When he was a young man and had just been bitten, he started having uncontrollable urges that ended with him having aggressive sex with his women. Initially, he attributed the urges to his newly acquired desire for sex, but once it had fully manifested in him, he had to feed. His first bite ended horribly and the victim died a death suited for the only enemy of a vampire, a witch. That woman died from the inside out, when her organs started rotting a few days later.

Unless he wanted to leave a trail of bodies, Thaddeus had to figure some things out. He had to feed daily and more and more his cravings for blood became prominent.

Eventually, it was the only thing he craved when he was hungry. Nothing filled his needs for sustenance like the taste of blood did.

When Allison first bit him he had two other ladies and his sexual urges were satisfied with one, both or all of them. As his transition progressed, his sex urges became hunger pains and he needed to feed before having sex. That's when he came up with the idea of more women to satisfy him.

He didn't want to be different and certainly did not want to harm humans. He learned as long as he did not bite into their vein and did not feed on them longer than 20-30 seconds at a time, no harm would come to them. The most important thing was he should not feed on a human more than twice a month. As long as he followed those guidelines for feeding, humans would be fine.

Thaddeus thought he could use his girls to feed on, which he could, but he didn't have enough of them to last him a month of feeding. So he sat out to get 30 women to feed on, in order to bring no harm to either of them. He would feed on them, bringing them to a euphoric state before he would have sex with them and each one of them was madly in love with Thaddeus Gotdoe.

Thaddeus had a way with women naturally, but with him becoming a vampire, everything about him was magnified. His conversation already was above average and the way he put his words together was so simple that it made the women he spoke with, giddy with excitement.

Then there was his sexual prowess, which is where any woman in his bed felt his power. She had already been mentally seduced and all of her inhibitions had been released, before he had sex with them. Each of them so willingly did what he wanted until he only had to look in the direction of the fruit bowl and they'd race to get a piece of fruit.

Pleasing Thaddeus was their only desire and as long as they did, he pleased them in many ways other than sex. He was the ultimate romantic date; refined, well educated, charming, charismatic, and had enough conversation to keep a date occupied for an entire evening. He was well versed in geography, although he hadn't traveled abroad. It was as if he'd seen many of the countries he spoke of.

Right now, he was going to meet with Allison for lunch. This meeting was to see if it would be feasible for her to move back in with him. Since she had been gone, Thaddeus had acquired a lot of property and she had gained a lot of financial skills from being involved in her husband's business transactions. It seemed a partnership like no other could be.

Throughout the early 30s, Thaddeus bought several apartment buildings and the old Sears office building in South San Francisco. In the latter part of the decade he took off from his work and went on several long vacations. His idea was to live off of his earnings for a while and not get too wrapped up in trying to acquire everything he saw.

He looked at his pocket watch and decided it was time to go to Jonelli's and meet with Allison. He drove his big, shinny Cadillac downtown and parked with the valet. He got out and told them he wouldn't be long. Thaddeus was never the nervous type, so he went right into the establishment and surveyed the dining room area, looking for Allison.

When he didn't see her, he headed to the bar for a cocktail and to his surprise Allison sat in a corner booth, with his favorite drink at the table waiting on him.

"I see you have not forgotten what I drink."

"What else would a vampire drink, except a Bloody Mary, which has real blood in it?" she asked seductively.

The way Allison responded, right away Thaddeus saw this was going to be a night of mental chess. He knew she knew if she wanted to get closer to him, she had to divulge secrets she hadn't told him. So she was going to see if she could use that to her favor. Thaddeus' need to know all he could about vampires made him read everything available and he'd found out some disturbing things that needed confirmation.

Before getting to the point, he had to play some of the games Allison had on her mind to play. They ordered a crab cocktail appetizer for two and when it arrived, Allison dipped her finger in the sauce and reached it up to Thaddeus' mouth. He hesitated, before letting her place her finger on his tongue. Thaddeus had to stay on his toes, because she was going to try to capture him any way she could.

The thing about Allison is she would not tolerate having a weak man. She would continue to try to make Thaddeus go for one of her ploys or tricks-which sticking the tip of her finger with one of her K9s and somehow getting him to suck it would prove him vulnerable to her ways. She probably would try to kill him after she made him look weak making such a mistake.

Thaddeus had already read about this and knew to have an olive on his tongue, which he had and planned to keep in his mouth throughout this date. The way he played it, even if she

did have blood on the tip of her finger the olive would be an antitoxin for it.

She smiled when she noticed his hesitation and said, "Don't worry. I know you are sharper than that. I am here to make you feel the way my King should feel . . . and that's totally satisfied. How many women does it take to satisfy you?"

"I guess I have 23 now and if I have them all in a three week period, maybe the last one will satisfy me. Then there is you . . . you're the only woman who can give me the passion I need correctly. I envy you in a way. You being able to do some things to me other women cannot do."

"Why envy me? You know I am not your regular woman. I am Allison Vimpyre, descendant of Alexander . . ."

"Woman desist! I will not fall prey to your vixen ways. I know not to allow you to recite your claim to your family's clan. This is a way to make me accept your authority over me and my world as it is now. You will have to be much more clever and conniving than that."

"This is why you excite me so much, Thaddeus Gotdoe. Your ability to thwart my attempts to show myself you are not worthy of my all, is simply a fucking aphrodisiac for me. Let's go now," she asked coyly.

"You do make me want to take you and do things to you I have only dreamed of doing . . . but I also know if you can get me to change or alter my evening with you, it puts you in the position of authority. Now, we can't have that; or can we baby?"

Allison stared at Thaddeus, but he slightly looked off to her ear, so that she did not gain a full gaze. After about 10 seconds, she leaped across the table and began kissing him. He tried to restrain her, but she had enough strength to force him to kiss her and when he did, she turned into butter in his hands.

After their embrace Thaddeus asked, "Can we order now?"

"Yes my King. We can order now," she said fully amped up, nostrils flaring and breathing hard as she stared at him looking at the menu.

Suddenly, Thaddeus looked up and caught her glare and held it long enough for Allison to submit to him. He then telepathically told her to salt his crab cocktail and she obeyed. Neither of them would ever tire of these dances, because it was the most erotic thing they could ever do together.

By now Thaddeus was just as 'ready' as Allison was, but to be a true King, your time is the only time that is important, so he could not rush any of their interaction before going to bed with her. He sat with an expression of satisfaction on his face that told Allison exactly what she was in for.

John Dickson

Illustration by Joe Geran: Brother Deacon Man

DOO WOP DAZE DANCE

Every time I hear a note of a song I remember from my teen years I wish I could return to all of the sweetness

of my innocence. Man! I still remember those summer time 25 cent socials, the blue lights barely illuminating

the darkest corners of our youth, the full punch bowl, the cream cheese on crackers, potato chips and salted

peanuts and how finally, one year, it became easy for me to place my fingers into the warm moist palms of the

eager girls who sat through song after song waiting for my invitation. There I was finally, iridescent suit, Nehru

collar, pegged pants, pointy-toed shoes. I gathered them into my arms and felt their warmth burning all resolve

to be mama's good girls as they pressed themselves to my lithe body. The slow music set it's delicious pace

and by the first crescendo they'd be riding my thigh like rag dolls ablaze. It was as if I danced with all of them

simultaneously. Damn! Desire was a sultry voice singing the words of the Chantels from the 45-RPM record on

the turntable behind the refreshment table. The silence that hugged the air when the song's last syllable ended was abbreviated by the soft scuffling of feet returning to their seats. The muted thank you's and quiet laughter

between guys and the whispered words and giggles between girls made the next song's beginning notes

evocative and deliriously wonderful as the night's heat stirred the passion of fast dances we thought we'd

invented.

George Edward Buggs

Upright Bass
for Dave Hay

"I'm the bass in your room," he says
grinning and squeezing his eyes closed,

He catches his breath, arranging his shoulders
just so and humming a little, though softly,

thinking his center is wood and open
and ready to thunder,

to oscillate, to bleed and get down
to it. He steps into the morning air,

locomotive, composed, sunny
and fabulously framed, opening tones,

walking just ahead of his steps, pressing
time and making it work. He is the motion,

the bottom, the riff at the start, the pulse down
under. "I'll be your bass, baby," he says,

turning it around: foundations aflame.

Susan Booker Morris

The Vampires Do the Ring Shout Down By the River

////By Peter J. Harris////Copyright 2016

NOTE: Taken from **THE VAMPIRE WHO DRINKS GOSPEL MUSIC:**

STORIES OF SACRED FLOW & SACRED SONG/BY PETER J HARRIS

... five interlocking stories ... written with the eloquence of a poet, the joyfulness of "Richard Pryor schooling Dracula on a midnight stroll," and ignited by a title story first published by an inspired Terry McMillan in her seminal anthology of African American short stories, Breaking Ice. www.blackmanofhappiness.come/shop

STORY NUMBER FOUR: "THE VAMPIRES DO THE RING SHOUT DOWN BY THE RIVER" ... It's dusk on an autumn day down by the Potomac River. Sechaba's dead body, CD player attached to his waist and blasting Aretha's "Amazing Grace" LP into his ears, lay on Gone Ground Found — a mound of earth from Sechaba's west African birthplace. LaTeisha Yvonne conducts the Ritual of Beginnings that she hopes will rejuvenate their First Ambassador and lead to final revenge on Candace and her murderous cohorts, now including Candace's lover Tony Brown, who's developed the Groove Adaptation Theory and asked his father figure, Blues Magic Man Junior Baby, to record the mix tape that they hope will be the ultimate weapon against the vampire who drinks gospel music.

"Lay his body down here on this holy ground."

The vampire's voice broke. Tears welled in her eyes. She watched the six bearers gently carry the body of Sechaba, their Saint, their Originator, and lay him delicately in the recess of the earth packed into the casket.

Not just any ground. This was *Gone Ground Found* — earth from Schaba's birthplace, a tiny suburb of the ancient city of *Ilé-Ifè* in west Africa. Earth he'd walked as a new vampire of the Mother

Coven, whose first lessons — difficult lessons, which he'd resisted — taught him the value of citizenship and service, *not* blood, *not* satisfying his hunger. Earth which absorbed the libations of his teachers, who slowly revealed the secrets of life-and-death lessons to a head-strong, arrogant initiate in his 30th year, who'd boldly sought out the coven so that he could gain the power that came with the blood hunger. Earth that was muddied by the blood he willingly spilled during skin-cutting manhood rites that tested his eagerness with pain. Earth containing the bone marrow of those initiates who died on their road to immortality. Earth from the region his Yoruban neighbors considered the epicenter of human beginnings. Earth, finally, that was brought over in the early 1800s when T'Shapa and Kepoka were sent to search for Sechaba. Earth kept uncontaminated on the coven's Georgia sea island sanctuary since that time. Earth used by Sechaba to reconnect himself with the ancestral home to which he could never return, once he developed his indispensable craving for African American sacred music.

He could never go home. There was no sound to feed him like the moan, the chorus of the African American Spiritual and the gospel music that grew from it. There was, indeed, the call and response at home, yes, and the harmonies, the grounding in multiple rhythms and percussion.

But after so many generations, Sechaba's desire could only be fed, his heart could only be comforted, his being could only be fulfilled, when washed and nourished by music filtered through the distinctive African-American genius. Sechaba could only survive on the magic drone of men singing out the location of the insurrection meeting, or singing out the promise of Heaven's salvation. He could only be recreated by the hypnotizing wail of the women timing the arrival of their flight from enslavement, or wailing passionately about their Savior's perfection.

The Mother Continent, for Sechaba, became the ancient mound of earth into which he shed his tears, when the sorrow of separation overwhelmed him, into which he slammed his fists in frustration over his blood curse, and his lust for the most beautiful music he'd ever heard.

Gone Ground Found — when he felt lost in eternity, split from everything and everyone, except the humans he chose to join him as one of the creatures of dependence.

Now, at dusk on an autumn day on a silent tract of land kissed by the Potomac River, Sechaba lay again on his holy ground.

He was dead. Really dead. He could not hear Aretha singing through the earphones of the portable compact disc player attached to his waist band. Aretha's "Amazing Grace" LP was his favorite among the modern sacred music.

He was dead. Really dead. He did not know that T'Shapa and Kepoka were here to help bring him back to life. They had kept their promise, after being elected by coven members, to rescue Sechaba's body from his murderers.

He was dead. Really dead. Sechaba could not feel the mental presence of the members of the Council of Caretakers and their sober dedication to overseeing the Ritual of Beginnings.

He was dead. Really dead. But lying on African soil, Sechaba was surrounded by a circle of the living dead. They could hear the music, smell the river, feel the psychic passion from their coven mates far away on a Georgia island in the Atlantic Ocean.

The members of the circle on the Potomac could even hear — in their deepest memories — the singing and praying of enslaved men, women and children, formed hundreds of years ago into rings of their own.

In their modern circle, the vampires could hear their ancestors shouting a departed loved one off to Paradise. The vampires could hear voices that gave balm to souls even more tortured than their own, voices that sent messages or answered prayers sung from another camp across this very river.

And the vampires inhaled the voices they heard echoing from the past. The vampires absorbed the life-affirming dedication of these old voices. The vampires sifted the voices between them, distilling the undecayed power, the raw determination, the timeless *let's get it on*!

The vampires became Aretha's choir, and did their own ring shout down by the Potomac River. Sechaba's children sang wordlessly, but it made the compact disc player glow, and Aretha got louder in their ears, uncovered by technology, but open to the throbbing reverberations of the music emanating from their Father's vibrating corpse. Sechaba's children sang wordless, this evening, to charge the air, the ground, the water, the past, present and future with the electric intention and renewal of their ancestors' voices.

Now that a steady hum had wrapped up the circle, The Ritual of Beginnings started in earnest. They were invisible to human eyes. The time had come for Roll Call.

There was a click.

"Damn, when Sony planning to make a reversible, portable CD player?" *LaTeisha Yvonne*, Council chair, said with exasperation.

One of the bearers, who'd been standing outside the circle, rushed to Sechaba's side. She quickly reset the CD player so it began playing "Precious Memories" again into Sechaba's deaf ears.

After members of the Renewal Group took a breath, and again tuned themselves to each other, to their mission, and to all the music in the air, Roll Call began. Introductions warbled on the sound of rhythmic voices:

"*LaTeisha Yvonne*, current chair of the Council of Caretakers, present and ready to sacrifice my everything for rebirth, this evening."

"Hakim, Council Second. Present and ready to dedicate my being to the never-ending Sacred Flow and Sacred Song."

Adela, present for re-creation, and prepared to rejoice when the light flutters into eyes opening on the Next Becoming."

"Sombe, present for re-creation and prepared to feel when touch returns to the Master's fingers."

"T'Shapa, present in grief and hope, in death and life ... committed to ensure that this misty instant becomes the sacred hour of rebirth."

"Kepoka, present in vacuum and sound ... ready to sing the song that fills up the emptiness with the melody of gratitude."

Outside the circle, the bearers did not speak.

Speech, in any event, gave way to the humming and movement. Ring members shuffle-stepped to the right, in a counterclockwise direction, clapping. They sent American dust flying into the air around the African vampire.

Aretha's heroic voice — "I'm climbing higher mountains/trying to get home" — swelled into the air and the ring dipped faster. Feet pounded to the ancient beat in the ancient style. Time meant nothing. It froze. It passed.

Until *LaTeisha Yvonne* sensed the moment to speak.

"We got obligations, this evening. Can I get a witness?"

The hum testified. The ring continued its orbit.

"Somebody saying *Rescue Me*, this evening. Do you hear?"

They did and dipped in affirmation.

"Deep waters cover our faces, this evening. We got strong swimmers?"

They raised their arms and clapped hands like splashing waves.

"The ring of protection is strong, this evening. Who ready to step inside the ring?"

"I am," T'Shapa said.

She stepped forward in time to the humming and shuffling and stood next to Sechaba's body.

"I say ... the ring of protection is strong, this evening. Who ready to step inside the ring?"

"I am," Kepoka said.

He stepped forward in time to the humming and shuffling and stood next to Sechaba's body.

"Love burns in our blood, this evening. Who love mean life?"

"My love mean life!" the vampires in the ring shouted in harmony. "My love mean life!"

"Somebody need your love, this evening. Who share their love?"

T'Shapa kneeled next to Sechaba's body and the ring droned encouragement.

"Blood contain your love, this evening. Who share their blood?"

Kepoka lay on the body of Sechaba. T'Shapa lay on Kepoka.

The ring found a new time to keep — double-dip and soul clap — as "Oh, Mary don't you weep" leaked into the lightless night.

"Remember when touch changed your world, this evening. Who remember the touch of new beginnings?"

Fangs bared, T'Shapa bit Kepoka's neck and clutched his back with intimacy and passion born from centuries of friendship and love. And Kepoka bit Sechaba and clung powerfully to his *father murderer savior*, as T'Shapa's blood and Kepoka's blood coursed into Sechaba.

The ring slid rhythmically to the right. The vampires clapped and hummed the sound of the CD choir singing "You got a friend."

Aretha flew like a magic genie.

Time meant nothing. It froze. It passed.

Until the blood, embrace, love, anger, humming, stepping, and clapping drew down the moon's light, and lit up the ground alongside the Potomac River.

Time meant nothing. It froze. It passed.

Until the battery-powered voices faded beneath the voices from the ring. And the vampires heard the faint echoes of older, invisible voices singing the historical wish for deliverance and defiance.

Time meant nothing. It froze. It passed.

Until Sechaba's eyes fluttered and opened in delirium and confusion — *could I be in an African hiding place of love and connection?* — and he reached reflexively to press T'Shapa and Kepoka into his body, feeling their blood pulsing into his mind. Sechaba strained his head upward to Kepoka's neck and bit, with the desperation of a being see-sawing between life and death. He bit Kepoka and reconnected with the man and woman he robbed of their mortality more than a century ago. Feeling Sechaba's movements, T'Shapa disconnected from Kepoka and bit Sechaba herself.

Jolted by the inspiration, the ring dipped exceptionally deep and clapped their hands as one. In their circular connection, they moaned as they witnessed the love, the blood, the circulation, death, life and immortality of the three who clutched on *Gone Ground Found* in a casket down by the Potomac River.

Time meant memories. It reversed. It revealed.

Until the vampires in the ring shared a vision showing how Sechaba, T'Shapa and Kepoka....

Kepoka, the griot, whose mastery of history and music made him more beautiful in the eyes of T'Shapa, the teacher of children, the woman of liberation .... They had tired of the intensity of urban life in *Ilé-Ifè*. Realized that their bond was immortal and wanted to create a family in more serene surroundings. They were drawn to the mysterious town nearby called Ba-Elia Enin, so famous for its hospitality to strangers, its curious citizens with a reputation as lovers of art and beauty, its public sculpture, and commitment to educating its children. They saw the city as the sanctuary they needed, so they moved there and became satisfied keepers of its civilizing flame.

Only after Kepoka and T'Shapa had found their place and rhythm in the town could they sense deeper magic, an overwhelming magic. The eerie stillness that quieted birds at sunset, that hypnotized them and intensified their passion.

After a year in their new home, they became even more drunk on each other. Urgent for the pleasure each brought to the other. Never satisfied, ever adventurous. Until taking one another within their shelter was not enough. They entered each other on the grounds of their place of worship. Within earshot of the marketplace. In private places reached only after steady walks into quieter parts of the forest. They inhaled each other. Entered each other's bodies and each other's thoughts and dreams. Even more than they already knew, she became the woman who received his honor and passion. He became the man who received her devotion and passion.

And their love, already subject of coven and community praise, became irresistible to one particular vampire, an ambitious, arrogant, lonely vampire, with a voracious, elemental hunger for companionship but who respected no privacy. Sechaba was intoxicated by their gifts as individuals, the obvious inspiration between them. Kepoka's masculine tenderness made Sechaba miss his own humanity. T'Shapa's feminine power made Sechaba miss the touch of a remarkable woman. He spent his waking hours hovering in the shadows, whispering their names, until their names rustled in the thick leaves of the palm trees, until the temperature within the young couple increased, until he ached for their blood, for their individuality, for their communion. He convinced himself, *lied to himself*, that they *wanted* the immortality he offered. He projected his own cravings onto this couple, who knew nothing of Sechaba's existence. Sechaba ignored his coven's convenant with their human neighbors, which rested on a Prime Agreement:

Humans whom the undead sensed might make immortal companions had to be *inspired* to accept the living death.

Vampires were free to feed on bandits, unjust rulers, humans in violation of the code of *Ba-Elia-Enin*, which celebrated each resident's virtuosity in service to the *All and All*. Indeed, the city's code even *embraced* the evil, the unsavory, within each of us, the evil that human can do unto human. Recognized vampires, too, as mirrors of the human being's evil practice and potential. Literal blood suckers were viewed as the reverse reflection of an individual's humanity. But they could not randomly snatch lives.

Agreements had been made during the living past, the past that lived as part of Ba-Elia Enin's struggle to cultivate and confirm a tradition of Whole Living. Vampires would not be hunted indiscriminately. Vampires would not hunt humans indiscriminately. Rites of Passage, negotiations, culture-sharing, core values, proverbs, stories, were the mutual responsibility of human *and* vampire, according to the Agreements. Hungers, selfishness, greed, lies, manipulations were acknowledged as part of both world's endowments.

But Agreements had been made. Agreements that had kept the balance alive in Ba-Elia Enin and kept the tiny town attractive to newcomers like Kepoka and T'Shapa, kept democracy alive between mortal and immortal. But Sechaba could neither resist nor withstand his need for this magical human couple. And when he could no longer find satisfaction as voyeur of their extraordinary love, when he could no longer be fed by the steam rising from the intensifying sexual waters they stirred, he ignored the Agreements and exercised his hunger for power ...

Time meant memories. It reversed. It revealed.

... T'Shapa and Kepoka were making love when I took them. Locked in sweetness. Hidden from all eyes except mine in their special hiding place in the forest. I climbed on them both, pressing so they could not move. I bit Kepoka. As I fed on him, I slit T'Shapa's throat with the nail on my right pinkie. With my left hand, I wrenched his head and pushed it till his mouth covered her wound. In that manner, we became joined as no others could become joined ...

Imprinting the collective mind of the circle with uncensored images and understandings ... not *just* that Sechaba took K & Shapa as they made love for the last time ... linking them with each other by a volatile blend of anger, loyalty and rebellion that could never be matched by any who would become vampires in the Time to Come ... but *branding* the witnesses in the circle with the profound and disappointing realization that Sechaba, who had stood as the emblem of their dignity, and who had insisted on the elemental harmony between human and undead, was as tainted by impure hungers as they were.

Could his dependence, could his love, for the music and art be a mask? A curse?

Oh and Aretha wailed and wailed in synch with their agonized participation in the past, and in the present, as they were electrified by ever-rippling anger, loyalty and rebellion that circulated between Sechaba, Kopoka and T'Shapa, three vampires locked in a revivifying embrace down by the river.

Time meant memories. It reversed. It revealed.

Until the vampires in the ring relived Sechaba's mission to the New World ... learning that, in fact, Sechaba was actually banished and *fed into the Triangle Trade*, as punishment, as impotent witness to what happens when Agreements are not kept, when long-nurtured Balance is ignored for immediate gratification ... learning that, ultimately, after five generations, his coven had forgiven him, and decided to dispatch T'Shapa and Kepoka on a quest to return him to Africa ….

They homed in on Sechaba in 1829 at a Sunday night camp meeting in Virginia. Revealed themselves as he stood within a small congregation of men, women and children. A reunion that crackled with unresolved tension, as he opened his eyes on the two creatures he'd missed the most during his exile. Gazing at them in shock. Still stunned by beauty he'd craved then frozen through coercion. Humiliated that he had lacked the courage to risk their rejection. Shamed that he had lacked the eloquence to woo them as demanded by the Agreements to which his coven was bound.

Gazing at them 100 years later, and thousands of miles from where he'd last beheld them, Sechaba was flooded with joy and grief and vulnerability.

And Kepoka and T'Shapa were shocked that he'd *aged?*

A vampire aging beyond the moment at which his mortality was severed?

The ring of witnesses down by the river released a collective sigh of amazement and interrogation, only to discern the explanation via the memories unfolding from the nexus between Sechaba, T'Shapa, and Kepoka, locked in an umbilical embrace on Gone Ground Found.

When the Mother Coven voted to exile the young Sechaba, the rejection shook him to his core. He'd anticipated punishment for taking the beautiful couple. Anticipated that he'd be shunned for a time. He'd anticipated *tsk tsk tsk* from his leaders, vampire and human. But exile? Banishment? In his decades-old memory, no creature had been banished for taking a human. (Sechaba was nothing if not defensive, in his statement during his trial!)

But even he had not truly understood how extraordinary T'Shapa and Kepoka were to the ancient ones. Perhaps with their sensitivity, the blended uniqueness of their humanity, the expansiveness of their mutual love and respect, they would have eventually and ultimately *volunteered* to become vampires, so they could walk together until the earth rotated, wobbled and orbited no more. Perhaps they would have discerned just how special they could be if they *chose* eternity as granted by the Transformation.

But stealing their freedom of choice? Ambushing them as Kepoka moved within the willing body of T'Shapa? Violating the privacy of their intimacy to try and fill a hole in your own stubborn core? This was the essence of criminal behavior in Ba-Elia Enin! *Only* exile could accommodate such a violation. And only banishment into the machinery of enslavement, which would not kill Sechaba, could provide him with the visceral understanding and fundamental example of the worst that humans can inflict, when they choose to shred the Agreements governing the ideas of true civilization.

So he was ordered into the maw of slavery or face destruction. Of course Sechaba chose life in exile. At sentencing, he maintained his public face of bravery and bravado, although nodding with a smidgeon of atonement at the couple, who glowed within their transformation. But he glared at his judges. Eternity is a long time, his expression sneered, as he was marched into his new life to become the most unusual cargo ever shipped within the Atlantic Slave Trade.

In truth, however, Sechaba's façade began crumbling within seconds after his sentence was pronounced. And his sorrow deepened as he was escorted at night by vampire security to the coast on the Bight of Benin. He took some preverse pride that he wasn't walking in step with human prisoners and, especially, with human traders, whom his city's Agreements would have allowed to be taken at will. But it was only misplaced pride.

Upon seeing the ship, christened the *Ave Maria*, that would take him beyond the horizon, upon being handed over to a hypnotized captain who would bound and seal Sechaba within a storage container for the trip to Barbados, and then by pirates to South Carolina, the façade thoroughly evaporated. Entombed within the bowels of a sailing coffin, Sechaba ached for the life whose perfection he'd taken for granted. He felt his connection to Ba-Elia Enin seep out of him, replaced by an oppressive miasma thickened by the humidity of his prison, the creak of the ship's water-logged wood, and the languages, songs, moans, and vows of his fellow Africans.

Shock set in. He'd made the biggest mistake of his life taking T'Shapa and Kepoka.

Sadness set in. He'd taken for granted his belonging within the order of Ba-Elia Enin.

Surrender set in. He was no longer the brazen predator lazily tracking the daily lives of a couple whose scent nourished his imagination.

He was a prisoner.

He grieved so hard that he stonily allowed himself to be 'sold' in a midnight sale to a private buyer, barely resisting the urge to bare his fangs and slay everyone in the room. But for what use? He was even severed from the comforting mental connection with his Coven leaders. He released his sense of power, except for his gift to hypnotize, which ensured that he had a place to sleep during the day. He became for a time a night rider, a bounty hunter, roaming the countryside at night to round up runaways.

As if he would!

Instead, he helped runaways escape, directed them to communities of outlyers and maroon colonies, but he released hopes for his own freedom. Began a blood-fast that lasted for the first 20 years of his exile. As his hunger atrophied, the stress caused his skin to lose its suppleness, his human shell to show the passage of time, but in an accelerated manner. The lush hair on his head became stippled with gray, including a tuft of shocking gray just above his right eye. By the end of a generation, he looked to be a man in his 60s.

Only when he caught his reflection in the moon-lit pond where he rested with a family he was guiding toward a nearby Underground Railroad labyrinth, did his appearance stun him into the first steps of recoiling from his self pity. It was that evening, upon escorting the family to the array of caverns appropriated by the the brave railroad conductors, that he actually *heard* the music through which he'd sleepwalked for years.

The voices, quiet enough to sound like wind to the ears of bounty hunters, contained the invigorating, enlivening pulse of spiritual gratitude of beings intent on overcoming profound loss for the chance to open their eyes on their own truth. These voices began Sechaba's realignment with the Agreement of Ba-Elia Enin and his return to the continuum of grace among the transplanted Africans. These voices helped him regain his will to live. Helped him rejuvenate his metabolism, although his physical appearance remained fixed. Forever more, he would appear, to the eye of all who beheld him, as an elder, which is how T'Shapa and K found their maker, Sechaba, in the Virginina camp meeting. Connected again by an invisible and indivisible current created in Ba-Elia Enin, Sechaba felt elated to see them, and at peace. If these two were to be the instrument of my destruction, then at least I'll be destroyed by the two creatures who most had the right to end my existence. Sechaba, cradled within the voices of his American flock, not a vampire among them, not a one of them under his thrall, leaned back his head and revealed his throat to the vampires he had frozen in the prime of their lives.

Yes, yes, yes, if this were to be my final hour, let it be among the swelling moans of testimony of those who taught me through their survival that the real covenant is with life, with love for life, against the relentless pressures of violence in every form, from every direction, without regard for age, sex, complexion, or temperament.

K and Shapa gazed at Sechaba and could feel the change, how he'd changed … love brought them back …. Sechaba's humility brought them back … And they, so utterly close to their maker, witnessed and experienced within their marrow how the sacred music of America was feeding him … was sustaining him … was circulating within him, and so startled were T'Shapa and Kepoka that they held hands and slowly entered the gathering, almost sauntering. They nodded to the men and women, touched the children's heads, and were welcomed by the brush arbor congregation.

Sechaba remained still and resigned to the fate they brought with them. His knees buckled when Kepoka slipped his right arm into Sechaba's left arm, when T'Shapa slipped her left arm into Sechaba's right arm. They held him up. The three of them wept in communion and Agreement. Without threat or domination, T'Shapa and Kepoka conjoined through their touch with their maker, and learned of his expansion and transformation that flowed from the salvation provided by Sacred Black American Song.

Aretha sang "Wholy Holy," voice cornrowed into the sweep of a fingered harp, the angelic call and response of the Sweet Inspirations, and uplifted by sweeping harmonies of the Southern California Community Choir. She rocked the earth's foundation, uplifted the final phase of the ring shout down by the riverside. The vampires in the ring relived T'shapa and Kepoka's decision to remain with Sechaba in the Americas. Witnessed Kepoka's revelation that he, unlike Sechaba, could find nourishment in all music — the dance-hall banjo and fiddle, the lonesome-acre harmonica, and the bent-note guitar. The griot Kepoka, student of sound and conversation, sensed the common seed in the Spirituals and the secular, but not Sechaba, who had reached his transformation's constitutional limits, leaving himself vulnerable to Candace's ambush.

Time meant memories. It reversed. It revealed.

Until the vampires in the ring could see that T'Shapa understood Kepoka, gaining tolerance to some of the variations on the Root Rock. The teacher T'Shapa, student of knowledge and divination, took immediately to the throbbing musical genius of her human cousins. She became Sechaba's final guide to imbibing the food in their labor, their stories and their rituals, maintained in the face of systematic violation.

Time meant memories. Time meant nothing. It reversed. It froze. It revealed. It passed.

Until the vampires in the ring felt keenly the life flowing between Sechaba, Kepoka and T'Shapa. And time returned to normal, down by the river, as the three ritually entangled vampires unclenched abruptly from each other, spent.

The humming stopped. The stepping ended. The light faded. The CD player clicked off.

Black silence pulsated.

T'Shapa stood. Kepoka stood. Sechaba stood. They embraced solemnly, with welcome in their touch. No one else spoke or moved until they released each other. Sechaba stepped toward the ring members standing with their arms extended. *LaTeisha Yvonne* stepped out from the group. Sechaba grabbed her hands with tears of thanks in his eyes. *LaTeisha Yvonne* wiped away his tears and eased the headphones from his ears and hung them around his neck. She smiled.

"He here, yall! He here!" *LaTeisha Yvonne* said. "The Ritual complete. Reunited ... and it feel *so* good!"

It did feel good, until Sechaba was shown the videos and films based on his precious diaries. He was enraged, relived his death all over again. Candace. Candace. Candace. Her name burned. Even killing him was not enough, *for Candace*. Destroying his art, his music, his home was not enough, *for Candace*.

Now she exposed his life to millions of strangers. And her latest sacrilege would be shown tomorrow at midnight — although *that's* a nice touch, he admitted.

Reuniting will feel so good, with Candace.

I'll time my appearance to coincide with the climax of the film. I'll make an entrance, the horrifying grandness of which will make them stampede as if their worst nightmares had come alive.

Sechaba had indeed made his entrance grand. With T'Shapa, Kepoka and *LaTeisha Yvonne* at his side, he had tapped his deepest abilities at shape shifting to blend with the fabric of the movie screen. When the four vampires appeared, they drew on each other's powers to gather light from the projector until the three of them towered in mid-air above the audience, which included Candace. Their presence shocked the audience, but it did not stampede. Everybody thought it was part of the show.

Stopping the film was easy. Telepathically, Sechaba commanded the projectionist to pause the film. The audience thought the screen images were supposed to stop, while they watched what they thought was a holographic continuation of the story.

Threatening Candace — oh, I should have taken her immediately! — failed to frighten anybody, either. The audience applauded and encouraged Candace when she and her murderous co-conspirators dared pull out silver daggers in resistance. Shocked, he lost control of the projectionist. Even the darkness of the theater only heightened the crowd's enjoyment. They laughed at Sechaba's quips, missing entirely the danger the quartet of vampires represented.

No, Sechaba's determination to strike fear in Candace and her paying customers failed miserably. Then, to add dangerous insult to injury, Candace again ordered the playing of secular music of the most insidious — *jazz organ trio music*. Grounded in African Time, as Kepoka has been explaining for over a century, but lacking for Sechaba the essential spiritual nutrients.

Despite his boastful threats to Candace, that dreaded music stabbed directly into Sechaba, as piercing as the knives Candace and Shelby had used to kill him. Sending nausea and weakness and pain throughout him, causing Sechaba to slump pitifully onto T'shapa and *LaTeisha Yvonne's* shoulders. He drew on their tolerances, weakening them. The hateful rhythms did what their gleaming daggers could only hint. Sechaba was forced to de-evolve back into the screen on which his murder had been reenacted. He found enough will power to reconstitute himself backstage, along with T'Shapa and *LaTeisha Yvonne*, and they escaped out the back door. They literally ran from Cramton Auditorium down Georgia Avenue to the Green Line Metro stop. Away from that stinging organ music. They were frustrated to find that the Metro stop had been closed due to track repair.

Sechaba and T'Shapa and *LaTeisha Yvonne* leaned with a weary clang against the grate and were promptly approached by a street walker for that quarter. Only Sechaba's distress after the organ attack kept him from ending the man's life. Instead, the vampires simply bared their fangs in answer to his wine-breath request, and Homeboy moved off (although with some indignation that they was ganging up on him and taking his favorite spot for the morning rush hour).

There they rested, until Kepoka found them telepathically. Disappointed and dejected, Sechaba allowed T'Shapa and Kepoka and *LaTeisha Yvonne* to return him to the sanctuary they had purchased off the back roads of Rock Creek Park. There, Sechaba sat listening to Aretha's *Amazing Grace* LP over and over and over. In their new neighborhood, it was not a common sound heard past the midnight hour.

"Unh unh, no more Tony. My teeth are chattering already."

Candace laughed with her mouth full of Breyer's strawberry ice cream, waving off the heaping spoonful that Tony Brown held up to her lips. They sat on stools in the cozy Dea's market and deli right at Georgia Avenue and Harvard Streets, a stroll from the central quad of Howard's main campus. When Tony Brown found out how much Candace liked ice cream, he brought her over to Dea's where ice cream is dipped by hand from big brown cylinders in the freezer, dipped to the sizzling tune made by burgers or cheesesteaks idling on the grill.

Dea's became their spot. After her classes in the School of Communications. After he'd knocked off from making calls on a case at the Bond and Brown Detective Agency.

Since routing Sechaba at the premiere of "The Vampire Who Drinks Gospel Music" — Candace still marveled at how deadly that killer organ music had been — the anthropologist and the private eye had become an item. Much to the delight of James Bond and Marla, whose recent enjoyment of their respite from Tony's interruptions included a lovely Sunday night picnic on the hood of their Subaru Outback in the Panorama Room parking lot, city lights reflecting in their eyes and off the several goblets of wine they raised.

Oh, but now, Tony Brown, known for his dour glare, his Coffin Ed and Grave Digger Jones game face, was all smiles. Walking around the office talking about Candace said this, Candace said that. Talking about Candace and me going to this interview to promote the film, which was earning big bank. Oh yeah, Tony Brown was buying new clothes, all worn with his trademark African pouch around his neck, so he could style in style.

Also, Tony Brown and Candace Stallings were jointly outlining a book on Tony's Groove Adaptation Theory. Simply stated, which is almost impossible for the long-tongued Tony Brown, the G.A.T. suggests that since Black people had adapted their capacity to create art forms to accommodate shifting social challenges (challenges out of their control), it stood to reason that their art forms could be adapted — their frequencies changed, so to speak — to defend humanity from the threat of vampires who fed on Black Sacred Music as well as on blood.

So, for example, Spirituals. Adapted as a medium of salvation and subversion in the face of slavery, they could be updated to provide protection and warning against the evil of Sechaba and his coven of vampires. In addition, the elements of the Spirituals — passion, improvisation, faith, movement, and creative democracy — were available in all of the best *secular* Black music and popular forms of music *derived* from Black music. They could be reordered in unlimited ways, particularly now within the vortex of the Digital Age.

Therefore, Sechaba could be kept off guard and off balance and he could never find the nourishment which existed within the secular sound, even though he might recognize a given element as coming from *spiritual sounds*.

Got it?

James Bond and Marla were blank-faced after Tony's explanation.

"Uh, we'll read the book," Marla said.

"Even then, *I'll* be needing a tutor," James said.

Well, anyway, back to Deas:

"I finally got Junior Baby to give us some time tonight," Tony Brown said, just before eating the dripping spoonful that Candace had rejected.

Junior Baby was the blues singer and raconteur who gave Tony Brown his pouch in 1973, and who was a father figure for the detective. Tony had wanted Candace to meet him so they could discuss what happened at the premiere, G.A.T., and so he could get Junior Baby's blessing about Candace. Tony Brown was serious and Junior Baby was family. His godfather since his parents died when Tony was seven.

"You mean I'm finally going to meet Mr. Junior Baby?" Candace said, smiling and fingering a chunk of strawberry out the dish into her mouth. "All you've told me about him, I'm nervous about meeting him."

"With what you've endured since meeting Sechaba? Please...." Tony Brown said. "Besides, Junior Baby is so polite, even if he disliked you, you'd never know it. But he'll love you, just like ... I ... seem ... to ...."

Tony Brown looked into the ice cream. There, he'd said it, almost.

"Mr. Brown," she said softly, touching his forehead with the back of her hand. "I believe you have a fever and are talking crazy."

She spooned some ice cream and put it in her mouth. Raised his head, turned his face to hers, and kissed strawberry ice cream into his mouth.

"A spoonful of sugar helps the medicine go down, remember," she said.

She took her own fever.

"I seem to be feeling something like love myself."

They stared at each other for a hot chocolate minute, cream melting on each other's tongues. Tony cleared his throat. Candace put the correct change on the counter.

"What time is that meeting with Mr. Junior Baby, baby?" she asked.

"Why, midnight, of course," Tony Brown said. "It's a habit from his club days, when he slept all day and galavanted all night."

"Well, then," Candace said. "It *seems* we have some galavanting time of our own."

"It would seem so," Tony agreed.

They melted off the stools and walked out without saying goodbye to Mr. Dea, who stood smiling behind the counter. Tony lived closest, in a quiet brick house near Eastern Avenue, and that's where they seemed to be heading for a consultation before their meeting with Junior Baby to talk about vampires, gospel music, and tapes full of the sounds of protection and warning.

It's a good thing Junior Baby's house was full of cushioned, well-worn furniture, because Tony and Candace arrived for their appointment more than a little wobbly-legged after their, uh, brainstorming session.

They sat, stuffed as full as his couch, sipping sassafras tea with a hit of Jack Daniels, as Junior Baby sat in a chair across the coffee table picking his guitar along with a recording of Wilson Pickett's "634-5789." The song wound down, and Junior Baby kept chanking and got to improvising some lyrics to let the couple know they looked good to him, and to let Tony Brown know he thought Candace was good people. He closed with a delicious chord and got down to business:

"So...?"

Junior Baby could wind his way through the wonders and worries of a love affair, political conversation, or damn near any other topic, when he wanted to. But he could also cut right to the quick. It startled Candace, after his meandering hospitality, but Tony Brown was used to it and started straightforwardly.

"We got vampires in town who live off gospel music."

Candace looked at Tony Brown with wide eyes at his bluntness. What if Junior Baby thought we were crazy?

"I know," Junior Baby said. "I was at Cramton when they appeared and messed up a perfectly good ending."

He pulled out his ticket stub from a pocket in his Guatemalan vest and waved it toward them. "Worth every penny, too!"

"Oh, Mr. Baby," Candace said. "I wish Tony had told me about you. I'd have given you a free ticket."

"Go on girl. I believe in paying my own way. I got a bird's eye view from the balcony. I seen how that organ music worked like a charm on all but one of them four blood suckers."

"Yes, yes, I noted how the other male vampire actually enjoyed the music," Candace said.

"That was Mr. Kepoka," Tony Brown said. "He and the elegant woman, ahem, vampire, hired us to track Candace so they could find Sechaba's body. Her name is T'Shapa. Weird couple."

"Maybe not," Junior Baby said. "Them three move like the Pips behind Gladys, the way I see it."

"And who was that round-the-way Queen Bee floating alongside them?" Candace wondered.

"No idea," Tony Brown said.

"Well, some way, somehow," Junior Baby mused, "that Mr. Kepoka got a understanding, and a way of feeling, to where it don't matter the kind of music, he got a ear to find the heartbeat."

"That makes him exceedingly dangerous, then," Candace said.

"And it challenges the root of the Groove Adaptation Theory," Tony Brown said.

"I don't know about no theory," Junior Baby said. "Except what little I learned times I sat down with one or the other music-maker I criss-cross during my years on the road," Junior Baby said. "But I can see how a vampire who can drink every type of music, along with all types of blood, could be a burr under the saddle.

"But that Sechaba fellow, he sure stuck on his gospel, and he's the HNIC, am I right Candace?"

She nodded.

"Yes. Sechaba's the heart and soul, having been the first to come to America from the Continent. I feel we definitely have to target him. He's bent on getting revenge against me, and I'm taking it as an article of faith that he's come too far to change his constitution now."

"Even after his rebirth?" Tony Brown asked.

Candace frowned. Junior Baby smiled.

"That's thinking, Tony, but we got evidence he couldn't handle that musical grits, grease and gravy yall played at the theater," Junior Baby said. "If he was gonna grapple with the scrapple, I'd a thought he would have hung right there and put some fear of, well, maybe not *God*, huh?—" Junior Baby chuckled — "the fear of *himself* and his kind into Candace here."

"So we really need to mix a tape that hits Sechaba so hard --" Tony started ...

"... That we hurt him in a way even worse than death," Candace continued. "If he thinks he'll have to face an ongoing, fluid and unpredictable medley of secular music, he will back off and leave humanity alone."

"We can return to the balance," Tony Brown said. "Remember he wrote about the ancient balance between his world and ours in his diaries."

"Good and Evil," Junior Baby said. "The crossroads where all us got to decide right from wrong."

Junior Baby got up and went over to his music collection. He took out a cassette from the complete recordings of Robert Johnson and cued up the song called "Cross Road Blues."

The scratchy guitar and voice wailed through the speakers. Asking for deliverance and guidance as he stood looking at the horizon as the evening sun goes down, searching the blues for an answer against the temptation in life to commit violence, to beat somebody out their rightful propers, to do wrong to a do-right woman, and protection when temptation overcomes him.

The tape played two versions of the song and the lonesome ending, where Robert Johnson sang he felt like he was sinking down, made it clear to Candace and Tony Brown that they were at the crossroads themselves. They were faced with recording music which could restore peace between humans and in humans. They were faced with danger that no ordinary love affair could withstand, nor should have to bear. They were faced with the responsibility of battling Sechaba, T'Shapa and Kepoka (and their feral homegirl, who would bite the latest *Jet* magazine's Beauty of the Week to get in on the kill!).

And in the balance: the lives of best friends.

Tony and Candace were faced with tests of their own fears of the unknown.

What if Kepoka's tolerance made him the leader?

What if Sechaba sent others to exact his revenge?

What if?

What if?

What if?

Junior Baby turned off the tape.

"That's why I love the Blues," he said. "Singer really only kicking against his own demons. Listener got to search his own self and figure out how to take care his own problems. That's what I always told you, Tony. Parents die. I can help. But you got to make your own peace.

"Vampires in D.C.—" he chuckled again — "*Real* vampires, not them fools up on Capitol Hill; well, I can help there, too, but Miss Candace, you got up on that bandstand once before. You gonna have to tune up, dig down and let Brother Sechaba know you belong in the spotlight one more time, look like to me."

"So...?" Tony Brown asked.

Junior Baby smiled and rubbed his stubbled chin. He sighed and surveyed his stacks of records, tapes and CDs. He picked up his guitar and started to strum, but decided against it. He stared at Candace and Tony.

"I believe I got a little something you can play at your next Halloween party."

Junior Baby started playing the "Cross Roads Blues."

Candace and Tony Brown held each other's hands. Strawberry ice cream had never given them a chill like they felt just then.

Author Bios

Tay Parker

Schauntte Hezekiah"Tay" Parker Jr. was born in Benton Harbor, Michigan, and raised in Grand Rapids, Michigan, and Venice "Ghost Town" California, where he was schooled at Sidewalk High, Venice High School and Santa Monica High School. Vowing to never work for "Charley", he mastered and was employed by the streets, then became a business man, owning Tays Playas Tattoos, one of the most successful tattoo shops in South Central Los Angeles for (17) seventeen years. From The Lobby to The Penthouse is the first book of his autobiography.

DENISE ST PATRICK-BELL, PhD:

Denise Richardson, is a native of Waterbury, Connecticut. She earned her bachelor and master degrees from the University of Connecticut and the Doctor of Philosophy (PhD) from the University of Arizona. She also completed postgraduate work at Florida Atlantic University.

Dr. Bell is an award winning educator, administrator, and community leader with a career that spans 30 years. She is the founder and president of the Genesis Group International Consultants (GACION) and a principal in Global Strategic Partnership Alliance. She is also a certified life coach.

Professionally, Dr. Bell has been a top-level corporate executive, school and college administrator, curriculum director, program developer, teacher, speaker, trainer, counselor, researcher, evaluator, technical writer, editor, human resource consultant and entrepreneur. She has conducted workshops and seminars on a variety of topics in the United States, the Caribbean, South America and Europe.

Both professionally and personally, Dr. Bell is committed to work that furthers the growth and wholeness of individuals while bringing about practical and positive results in their lives.

This is her first published biography. Look for her soon to be published book "Healing from Betrayal" in which she discusses the five sources of betrayal that can lead to emotional tearing, scarring, and crippling. Dr. St. Patrick-Bell is a resident of South Florida. Follow her on facebook.com/GAICONLLC.

KING E. CARTER

The author was born in Sawyerville, Alabama and raised in Ramona Gardens Housing Projects, in the Boyle Heights area of Los Angeles. He attended Abraham Lincoln High School, where he majored in Science and Foreign Language. Upon graduating from high school, he entered the

University of Redlands (1966-1970), majoring in Sociology, Philosophy, and History. After Redlands, he earned his MA Degree in Education at Claremont Graduate University (1970—1972). His formal educational studies ended at UCLA (Administrative and Policy Studies in Education), with additional courses taken at UCSD, CSULB, and CSUDH. His teaching experiences includes Ganesha High School in Pomona, California (United States History, African-American Literature, and Cultural Anthropology); the Los Angeles Community College District (African-American History, History of African Civilization, United States History, Humanities, Sociology, Critical Thinking, and Ethics; the University of Phoenix (General Education courses);, and, California State University, Northridge (Developmental Reading, Developmental Writing, Effective Composition, and Critical Thinking and Race). The author has over 44-years of teaching experience, and has administrative experiences as the Acting Director of Black Studies (University of Redlands), Regional Coordinator of TRIO Programs Training (Atlanta University), and as the Director of the Program for Accelerated College Education (PACE) with the Los Angeles Community College District. Formally retired from teaching, the author spends his time writing poetry, mentoring students, serving on the Ronald McDonald House Charities Future Achievers of America Scholarship program, and as a member of the Mayme Clayton Library and Museum Board of Directors.

PHILLIP B. MIDDLETON

Phillip B. Middleton was born August 10, 1947 in Rocks, Maryland and grew up in Atlanta, Georgia where he was educated through college. After serving two years in the U.S. Army as a military policeman, he attended Tennessee State University, and Southern Illinois University, and prospectively earned a M.A. and a Phd. in English. He then began to travel and teach abroad, first in Tripoli, Libya for two years; then in Niamey, Niger, for three years, and later moved to Bristol, England, and began to write full time. He has held Fulbright Fellowships in the Sudan from 1984-1987, in Romania, from 1995-1997, and in Syria for one year.

Susan Booker Morris

Susan Booker Morris is a native Illinoisan whose family moved frequently throughout her childhood. As a result, she became interested in and aware of cultures and cultural differences and how art expresses these differences. She began writing poetry at the age of 11 when she wrote a poem in response to her grandmother's death. She taught English Literature and Composition through the 80s and earned a PhD in Philosophy at Southern Illinois University in 1997. Currently, Morris is a Professor in the Humanities department at Ferris State University in Michigan where she teaches Race and Gender Theory, Film, Philosophy, and Eastern Religions. She is also a vocalist in the jazz ensemble Bluemonk, which performs in various venues in Michigan and is set to release a CD.

Azam Obidov

Aazam Obidov is poet and translator, one of the founders of the Creative Writing and Translation Club in Tashkent, winner of Ulughbek Fund's prize for poetry. He also gained BBC Uzbek Service's award for literature. He published more than ten poetry and translation books, including Tunes of Asia (anthology of contemporary Uzbek poetry in English); A Miracle is on the Way; and I leave You in Complete Boredom. Azam tries to become a bridge between contemporary Uzbek literature and World Literature. He attended creative writing programs, poetry and translation festivals in the USA, Germany, Sweden, Russia, India, Kazakhstan and Colombia

Kim Evans

K Evans is a native to Southern California with strong roots in her Malagasy heritage. The youngest out of eleven children has developed a unique writing style that incorporates her interest in Anthropology and culturalism as well as drawing on her personal spiritual beliefs. Ms Evans holds a M.S. in Forensic Psychology and B.A. in Criminal Justice Administration. She has worked in several of California's prisons for men and as a Detention Service's Officer in the Juvenile Justice System. Currently Ms Evans is honing her skills as a transformational speaker and talks to individuals of all ages and circumstances giving direction on moving through life's most challenging moments.

Peter J. Harris

Peter J. Harris is the author of *Bless the Ashes*, poetry (Tia Chucha Press), winner of the 2015 PEN Oakland Josephine Miles Award, and *The Black Man of Happiness: In Pursuit of My 'Unalienable Right,'* a book of personal essays, winner of a 2015 American Book Award. www.blackmanofhappiness.com/shop. Since the 1970s, Harris has published his work in a wide variety of publications, most recently in *Wide Awake: Poets of Los Angeles and Beyond*, edited by Suzanne Lummis; *Altadena Poetry Review: Anthology*, edited by Thelma T. Reyna, Poet Laureate of Altadena; and *Coiled Serpent: Poets Arising from the Cultural Quakes & Shifts in Los Angeles*, edited by Neelanjana Banerjee, Daniel A. Olivas, and Ruben J. Rodriguez. Since 1992, he's been a member of the Anansi Writers Workshop at the World Stage, in LA's Leimert Park.

Cecilia Manguerra Brainard

Cecilia Manguerra Brainard is the award-winning author and editor of nineteen books, including the novels *When the Rainbow Goddess Wept* and *Magdalena*. The books she edited include, *Fiction by Filipinos in America*, and *Growing Up Filipino I and II*. Cecilia has also written a novel with four other women entitled, *Angelica's Daughters, a Dugtungan Novel*.

Her work has been translated into Finnish and Turkish; and many of her stories and articles have been widely anthologized.

Cecilia has received a California Arts Council Fellowship in Fiction, a Brody Arts Fund Award, a Special Recognition Award for her work dealing with Asian American youths, as well as a Certificate of Recognition from the California State Senate, 21st District. She has also been awarded by the Filipino and Filipino American communities she has served. In 1998, she received the Outstanding Individual Award from her birth city, Cebu, Philippines. She has received several travel grants in the Philippines, from the USIS (United States Information Service). In 2001, she received a Filipinas Magazine Award for Arts. Her books have won the Gourmand Award and the Gintong Aklat Award.

She has lectured and performed in worldwide literary arts organizations and universities, including UCLA, USC, University of Connecticut, University of the Philippines, PEN, Beyond Baroque, Shakespeare & Company in Paris, and many others. She teaches creative writing at the Writers Program at UCLA-Extension.

She is married to Lauren R. Brainard, a former Peace Corp Volunteer to Leyte, Philippines; they have three sons. She has a website at www.ceciliabrainard.com and a blog at cbrainard.blogspot.com

Martin Perlich
Author - Producer - Broadcaster

The author of the classic work "The Art of the Interview" (Silman-James Press (2007), writer, producer and broadcaster Martin Perlich has written screenplays and novels, poetry and documentary films. "The Wild Times," the first novel of his "Adequacy Quartet," was published by Empty Press in 2006. "The Self-Pity Chronicles" was published in 2011 by Empty Press. He has broadcast classical music, jazz and rock and roll, and amassed an unique archive of interviews: from Gore Vidal to John Adams, to Bill Evans.

His interview show "Martin Perlich Interviews" featuring Leonard Bernstein, Frank Zappa, R. Crumb, Pierre Boulez, Tom Waits and hundreds more, was syndicated nationally by WCLV/Seaway productions. The program won the New York International Radio Festival for two consecutive years. A copy of public TV documentary "Citizen Artist" is in the Smithsonian permanent collection.

Until leaving innovative LA public radio station KCSN, Martin was Program Director, responsible for all KCSN programming, which was named "Best of LA" by Los Angeles Magazine in 2006. In addition Perlich hosted an acclaimed daily classical and New Music show. He hosted and produced "ARF!!" (ARTS & ROOTS FORUM) the unique daily live interview series featuring major cultural figures, form Stacy Keach to Terry Riley to Sandra Tzing Loh to avant-garde playwright Murray Mednick, as well as dozens of arts figures: writers, directors, choreographers, and musical figures from Jazz, World music, and of course classical music, with many 21st century composers--known and unknown.

Perlich's early work was in music history. After studying with distinguished American composer Douglas Moore at Columbia University, he became, at 24, the first Intermission Host of the internationally syndicated Cleveland Orchestra radio broadcasts. Perlich worked closely with Musical Director George Szell as well as providing insightful interviews with Leonard Bernstein, Aaron Copland, Elisabeth Schwarzkopf, Isaac Stern and hundreds of others in his seven year stint.

As the 1960s became a cultural hurricane, Perlich was a pioneer in "experimental radio," continuing through the 60s into the 70's with interviews for WMMS in Cleveland and KMET in Los Angeles, featuring luminaries of that turbulent period: Jane Fonda, members of Panther Party and American Indian Movement, Dick Gregory, Lawrence Ferlinghetti, Isaac Asimov, Attica prisoners and eight memorable encounters with Frank Zappa and hundreds of other rock and experimental musicians.

In 1970, after Martin's second interview with Leonard Bernstein, the Maestro asked him to head a new production division he was proposing to Columbia Records, which Bernstein invited Perlich to head, overseeing the production of film and video of Bernstein's conducting projects. In addition Martin would be tasked with finding or writing "a second West Side Story" as well as text for the new Mass that he was composing for the opening of the Kennedy Center in Washington, DC. When Columbia balked at funding the Leonard Bernstein Division, the Maestro left the label for Deutsche Grammophon for whom he produced a legendary recorded legacy. As Bernstein left for Vienna, Martin came to LA.

In a rare display of versatility Perlich joined the staff of leading West Coast progressive rock station KMET, where he hosted "Electric Tongue," a weekly interview show featuring major rock and arts figures. In 1975 Perlich became Creative Consultant of NBC-TV's weekly 90-minute "The Midnight Special," responsible for the acclaimed "Salute" segment, a regular documentary featuring major pop and rock music figures: Jerry Lee Lewis, Aretha Franklin, Stevie Wonder, Loretta Lynne and others, in addition to writing, rehearsing and helping edit the history-making network show itself. In !998 he was honored by the Rock & Roll Hall of Fame for his pioneering contribution to experimental "progressive" radio

At PBS's KCET in Los Angeles and WNET in New York, Perlich developed and produced dramatic, music and documentary programming including: "Citizen Artist," "Hollywood 90," "Singer/Songwriter," (which he hosted) and "Informance." In 1985 he produced the seminar "Shooting for Change," focusing on socially responsible feature films, with panelists drawn from major studios and leading independent filmmakers. Then he founded Wilton Place Films, and developed (writing and producing) "The Trial of Ramona Africa" with Whoopi Goldberg under the aegis of American Playhouse and Channel 4 in London.

Perlich has written, produced and directed interactive video with Warner New Media (CD-ROMs: Brahms' A German Requiem; Carl Orff's Carmina Burana; and the vast interactive educational project "The Orchestra"); as well as "Taj Mahal: Like Never Before" for Private Music.

As an actor, Perlich has worked with legendary director Norman Corwin and with Jeff von der Schmidt and Southwest Chamber Music in Samuel Beckett's Cascando.

Perlich is the father of three, including actor Max Perlich, and currently lives in West Hollywood, CA.

Gloria Enedina Alvarez
Chicana poet/intermedia artist, playwright, librettist, literary translator and curator, presently teaches creative writing and works as a consultant in public schools, universities, libraries, museums, and art centers. Her literary/artistic efforts have been recognized by the CAC, National Endowment for the Arts, Cultural Affairs Department, City of L.A., COLA Award, Poets & Writers, Inc., among others. She has published and read widely in the U.S., Latin America and Europe. Her plays and librettos for opera, Los Biombos, Cuento de un Soldado/Story of a Soldier, El Niño, have been produced internationally. Her books of poetry in English and Spanish include La Excusa/The Excuse and Emerging en un Mar De Olanes. Her poetry has been published in various anthologies and numerous periodicals.

Maat em Maakheru Amen

Ma'at em Maakheru Amen is a <u>Brain Balanced</u> Kemetic High Priestess, Yoruba Initiate, author of the book: **<u>Whatz In Your Womb?</u>**, 10 year veteran Reiki Master/Teacher and Belief Management Counselor. She is also known to some as the Hiphop Reiki Master. She is the founder of the **<u>Ma'at Foundation, Inc</u>**, **<u>Soul Psychic Fair</u>**, and Groove Movement. She co-founded**<u>Being A Part</u>** with her husband, Yah-I Ausar Tafari Amen where they offer relationship and lifestyle advice. She specializes in releasing subtle and core energies stored as beliefs. She has traveled across the country speaking on Energy from an Afrikan and interactive perspective and has presented her seminar at the Congressional Black Caucus, Urban League Young

Professionals Group, as an opening speaker for KRS-One lectures, and the currently tours with Natural Hair Care Expo.

Now as the author of **Whatz In Your Womb**, Ma'at has focused her energy on clearing womb energy and beliefs in order to restore the true function and frequency of the womb in Black Women. Out of this movement, she has developed a technique called A.W.E. (Ancestral Womb Elevation), in which the participants identify and elevate the traumatized womb energy of their first enslaved ancestor. She is currently writing her 2nd book, Whatz Your Womb Thinking which deals with the introduction to the inner workings of the body, brain, personality, and soul, introduction to the brain of the womb and her various functions, understanding power versus light, being an analyzer versus a god, and the "real" activation of the god genes through brain balancing. For more information about Ma'at, visit WhatzInYourWomb.com or call 919-590-WOMB.

David Marquard
David Marquard is a writer and an assistant professor of English at Ferris State University in Big Rapids, Michigan. He teaches writing, rhetoric, and linguistics

Mark Thomson
Mark Thomson is a professor of Chemistry at Ferris State University in Big Rapids, Michigan, where, after being invited to find housing and employment elsewhere by Hurricane Katrina, he now teaches courses in General and Physical Chemistry, Biochemistry, and Fermentation. His more pleasurable pursuits involve his wife and their daughter of ten. When not otherwise engaged, he has long followed a multicultural, multilingual muse that now most often knocks on the door in the middle of the night in Spanish with a heavy Puerto Rican accent.

Susan Booker Morris
Susan Booker Morris is a native Illinoisan whose family moved frequently throughout her childhood. As a result, she became interested in and aware of cultures and cultural differences and how art expresses these differences. She began writing poetry at the age of 11 when she wrote a poem in response to her grandmother's death. She taught English Literature and Composition through the 80s and earned a PhD in Philosophy at Southern Illinois University in 1997. Currently, Morris is a Professor in the Humanities department at Ferris State University in Michigan where she teaches Race and Gender Theory, Film, Philosophy, and Eastern Religions. She is also a vocalist in the jazz ensemble Bluemonk, which performs in various venues in Michigan and is set to release a CD.

Erica K.B.
Erica is a Los Angeles native, now residing in central Virginia. She is a mother of one, a closet foodie and people appreciator. She describes herself as an old soul millennial with an eclectic taste in music and entertainment. Her favorite shows include Murder She Wrote and The

Golden Girls, and for that she is mighty proud. Outside of both her professional and writing career, Erica enjoys relaxing with loved ones and vibing with planet Earth.

GEORGE EDWARD BUGGS

George Edward Buggs received his B.S. degree in History from Hampton Institute (Virginia) and his M.A. in English (Creative Writing) from Brown University. While enrolled at Brown University he taught creative writing to undergraduates and he participated in the Rhode Island Council on the Arts' "Art's in the Libraries" program as a Creative Writing Specialist for the Roger Williams College's University Without Walls program at the Rhode Island Correctional Facility. He is a photographer and poet. His poems have appeared in many periodicals and small magazines including The Woodstock Seasoner, Iowa Review, Black Scholar, American Poetry, Evergreen Review, Black Lines, Black Creation, Pendulum, W.I.P., Obsidian, Saracen, The Providence Review, Pegasus, Ishmael, Kumanitu, Big Moon, B.O.P. (Blacks on Paper), and Image and Issues and Roxbury Literary Annual (Vol.1 and 2). He has published work in Broadside Press' Broadside Series (#51) and has had a volume of poems, **Music from the Middle Passage**, published by Cornerstone Press (St. Louis). In 1969 he received the Reader's Digest-United Negro College Fund's Creative Writer's Award for Poetry. In 1972 and 1973 he was a Bread Loaf Writer's Conference Scholarship recipient. He has given readings of his poems at several colleges and universities including Sarah Lawrence College, Hampton Institute, Oswego University and Brown University. His photography credits include the New England Black Weekly newspaper, Blackfolk, the Cambridge River Festival, and Channel 7/WNAC TV's Weekday program. He has exhibited his photographs at the Cambridge Public Library and Northeastern University. His writing activity includes the completion of FIVE- GRAND SURPRISE, a one-act play and LEGACY, a full-length three-act play. These plays were started while the writer was participating in ACT Roxbury's playwriting workshop, "Five Fridays and A Sunny Afternoon", conducted by playwright Ed Bullins in 2001 and 2002 in Boston, Massachusetts. He currently resides in Aiken, South Carolina and is engaged in digital photography and creative writing. His primary subjects are the equine activities for which Aiken is known. He has exhibited his photographic art in a number of local venues. They include The Aiken Center for the Arts, The McCormick Arts Center at the Keturah, (McCormick, S.C.), Equine Divine Art Gallery (Aiken), the South Side Gallery (Aiken), Aiken Office Supply, and The Aiken Spring Classic Horse Show (2007). His photos have appeared in the Aiken Standard, The Aiken Training Track brochure and The Thoroughbred Times, Equestrian Quarterly Magazine, Meybohm Real Estate Guide, Aiken Homes and Lifestyle Magazine, Dogwood Stable Newsletter, Aiken Polo Club Magazine, Whiskey Road Hunt Magazine and the Aiken Hounds Centennial Program also include his fine art photos. He received the Aiken Center for the Arts Board of Directors Award 2012 for his digital composite photo "Preserving Aiken's best"

John Dickson

John Dickson is an author and radio personality from Vallejo, CA. He received his Bachelor's and Master's degrees from Ashford University in Clinton, Iowa, and was featured in the film *American Pimp*. His books are: *Invention Man 1 & II, Time Will Tell, Thaddeus Van Gogh,*

Rosebudd, American Pimp, Fears, and Mothers He's Your Son. Dickson also has a radio show Ask Rosebudd. Askrosebudd.com askrosebudd@gmail.com.

Lola Rainey

Lola Rainey is an Arizona "Border" writer, educator and community activist. Her poems, prose and flash fiction, which can be found in literary journals and anthologies, reflect her Southwestern Afro-Mestizo cultural roots. "I am a creature of the desert. It is my source of inspiration," Rainy said. She is the author of two books: "Havasu Means Blue Water" and "The Rainy Season". Her prose play "American Haiko: Pain" was produced and presented at the 2016 Tucson Fringe Festival. The works published in Onyx are excerpts from a manuscript in development entitled, "Darkness In The Margins".

Pam Ward

Pam Ward is a graduate of UCLA, a recipient of a California Arts Council Fellow in Literature and New Literary Arts award , has had her poetry published in numerous journals, is the author of the novels, Want Some Get Some,Bad Girls Burn Slow, a book of poetry, Jacked Up, and has edited five anthologies.She has been an artist in residence for the city of Los Angeles and Manhattan Beach, was a board director for the Beyond Baroque Literary Arts Foundation, has served and worked for many community arts and health foundations and is the owner of Ward Graphics, as well as running her own publishing house, Short Dress Press.

D Hideo Maruyama

D Hideo Maruyama currently teaches English at El Camino College Compton Education Center. He currently teaches English at El Camino College Compton Center, and holds a MFA in Creative Writing from Long Beach State, and still believes in the long poem, but now is exploring travel writing and playwriting. He has a long history with nonprofits both in the arts and in relief work.

He was the President of Aisarema during the 1990s to early 2000s (Amerasia spelled backwards) which produced yearly poetry readings and an Asian Pacific American Arts journal called dIS*orient Journalzine. He was also the Editor in Chief of this Los Angeles Based journal for many years, which published a number of APA writers like Velina Hasu Houston, Monique Truong, Amy Uyematsu, Philip Kan Gotanda, and Elaine Kim. Under his watch, he created dIS*courses, which was a project of dIS*orient to partner poets from different communities to create unified poetry/fiction collections.

In 2004, he was a guest curator for a writer/visual artist collaborative project called City Dialogues at Los Angeles Municipal Arts Gallery at Barnsdall Art Park. This project developed collaborations between such writers as Gerald Locklin, Ray Zepeda, Michael Datcher and Jenoyne Adams with visual artists.

As a playwright, he has been a member of East West Players David Henry Hwang Writer's Institute, which resulted in a number of staged readings of full length plays: *Accidental Nexus* (2003), *Sato's Dream in Blue* (2006), *Time After Time-A Catalogue of Traumatic Events* (2007), *IFDD Station* (2009) and *Double Exposure* (2013). He is currently a member of The Company of Angels Theater's playwriting group, and he has staged two short plays as part of COA's LA Views short play series: *LA to Little Saigon (2014),* and *Nails of Little Saigon (2015).*

In 2010, he received a Fulbright Hays Group Project Abroad grant to research in Vietnam and Cambodia. He recently was an Assistant Editor for a collection of Vietnamese Boat People stories.

Emory Holmes II

Emory Holmes II is a Los Angeles based novelist, playwright, poet, children's story writer and journalist. His news stories on American crime, schools and the arts have appeared on the pages of the San Francisco *Chronicle*, the Los Angeles *Times*, the Los Angeles *Sentinel*, The Los Angeles *Daily News*, The New York *Amsterdam News*, *Los Angeles Magazine, Essence, CODE*, the *R&B Report, Written By* magazine, *The New York Times* wire service, and other publications.

He has scripted scores of radio programs for national syndication, including the 3-hour documentary on the Civil Rights Movement, *King from Atlanta to the Mountaintop*, which has been re-broadcast nationally since 1985. He was twice editor of the African-American men's monthly, *Player's* magazine, during the 70s and 80s, for whose parent company, Holloway House, he wrote two novels, *Black Rage* (1975) and *Sunday Hell* (1982). *Heavy Mr. Smevvy*, (1974) and *Justoka*, (1977), his two children's books, were published and distributed by his family press, Just-In-Tyme Publications. His crime stories have appeared in three anthologies, *The Cocaine Chronicles* (2005), *The Best American Mystery Stories 2006*, and *Los Angeles Noir* (2007). His story, "Dangerous Days," was translated into French and republished in Paris by Asphalte books in 2010; and this story, along with his short story "aka Moises Rockafella," has been dramatized by Amazon and brought out as an audio book for Audible in Dec. 2014. His essay, "Founders' Promise is Fulfilled" was the Page One story for the L.A. *Daily News* on Jan 20, 2009 -- the day of Barack Obama's inauguration. He has just expanded his short story "Dangerous Days," into a crime novel, titled "Dangerous Dayz."

Find out more at

Jasmaya.com

www.ingramcontent.com/pod-product-compliance
Lightning Source LLC
Chambersburg PA
CBHW080554090426

42735CB00016B/3237